Reforming Agricultural Commodity Policy

AEI STUDIES IN AGRICULTURAL POLICY

Reforming Agricultural Commodity Policy

Brian D. Wright and
Bruce L. Gardner

The AEI Press

Publisher for the American Enterprise Institute
WASHINGTON, D.C.

1995

Available in the United States from the AEI Press, c/o Publisher Resources Inc., 1224 Heil Quaker Blvd., P.O. Box 7001, La Vergne, TN 37086-7001. Distributed outside the United States by arrangement with Eurospan, 3 Henrietta Street, London WC2E 8LU England.

Library of Congress Cataloging-in-Publication Data

Wright, Brian.
  Reforming agricultural commodity policy / Brian D. Wright, Bruce L. Gardner.
      p.   cm. — (AEI studies in agricultural policy)
    "Publisher for the American Enterprise Institute."
    Includes bibliographical references and index.
    ISBN 0-8447-3906-5 (cloth : alk. paper)
    1. Agriculture and state—United States.   2. Produce trade—Government policy—United States.   3. Agricultural laws and legislation—United States.   I. Gardner, Bruce L.   II. American Enterprise Institute for Public Policy Research.   III. Title.
IV. Series.
    HD1761.W74   1995
    338.1'873—dc20   95–17821
                                                                            CIP

ISBN 0-8447-3906-5 (alk. paper)

1   3   5   7   9   10   8   6   4   2

THE AEI PRESS
Publisher for the American Enterprise Institute
1150 17th Street, N.W., Washington, D.C. 20036

Printed in the United States of America

Contents

PRACTICAL POLICY ALTERNATIVES FOR THE 1995 FARM BILL

Bruce L. Gardner

List of Figures

Foreword

Reforming Agricultural Commodity Policy is one of eight volumes in a series devoted to agricultural policy reform published by the American Enterprise Institute. AEI has a long tradition of contributing to the effort to understand and improve agricultural policy. AEI published books of essays before the 1977, 1981, and 1985 farm bills.

Agricultural policy has increasingly become part of the general policy debate. Whether the topic is trade policy, deregulation, or budget deficits, the same forces that affect other government programs are shaping farm policy discussions. It is fitting then for the AEI Studies in Agricultural Policy to deal with these issues with the same tools and approaches applied to other economic and social topics.

Periodic farm bills (along with budget acts) remain the principal vehicles for policy changes related to agriculture, food, and other rural issues. The 1990 farm legislation expires in 1995, and, in recognition of the opportunity presented by the national debate surrounding the 1995 farm bill, the American Enterprise Institute has launched a major research project. The new farm bill will allow policy makers to bring agriculture more in line with market realities. The AEI studies were intended to capitalize on that important opportunity.

The AEI project includes eight related topics prepared by recognized policy experts. Each study investigates the public rationale for government's role with respect to several agricultural issues. The authors have developed evidence on the effects of recent policies and analyzed alternatives. Most research was carried out in 1994, and draft reports were discussed at a policy research workshop held in Washington, D.C., November 3–4, 1994. The topics include investigation of

- the rationale for and consequences of farm programs in general
- specific reforms of current farm programs appropriate for 1995, including analysis of individual programs for grains, milk, cotton, and sugar, among others
- agricultural trade policy for commodities in the context of recent multilateral trade agreements, with attention both to long-run goals of free trade and to intermediate steps
- crop insurance and disaster aid policy
- the government's role in conservation of natural resources and the environmental consequences of farm programs
- farm credit policy, including analysis of both subsidy and regulation
- food safety policy
- the role of public R&D policy for agriculture, what parts of the research portfolio should be subsidized, and how the payoff to publicly supported science can be improved through better policy

The present volume, authored by Professors Brian D. Wright and Bruce L. Gardner, focuses attention on the basic farm commodity programs. Wright begins by challenging the rationales usually offered for U.S. farm programs. After finding no solid economic or social basis for most government involvement in agriculture, he argues for dismantling current programs. In the second half of the volume Gardner considers how we should go about revising the current programs if we are starting from an existing policy framework. Thus, he considers reforms that would be positive in the case that it is not feasible to make radical changes in 1995. Gardner examines policies commodity by commodity and finds that the approach of lowering the current target prices to the expected level of market price would provide some income support to commodity producers while dramatically reducing market distortion and budget exposure for the government. Both Wright and Gardner challenge supporters of the status quo and provide guidance to those looking for reform of the farm program in 1995 and beyond.

Selected government policy may be helpful in allowing agriculture to become more efficient and effective. Unfortunately, most agricultural policy in the United States fails in that respect. In many ways, the policies of the past six decades have been counterproductive and counter to productivity. Now, in the final few years of the twentieth century, flaws in policies developed decades ago are finally becoming so obvious that farm policy observers and participants are willing to consider even eliminating many traditional subsidies and regulations. In the current context, another round of minor fixes is now seen as insufficient.

In 1995 Congress seems ready to ask tough questions about agricultural policy. How much reform is forthcoming, however, and which specific changes will be accomplished are not settled and depend on the information and analysis available to help guide the process. Understanding the consequences of alternative public policies is important. The AEI Studies in Agricultural Policy are designed to aid the process now and for the future by improving the knowledge base on which public policy is built.

CHRISTOPHER DeMUTH
President, American Enterprise Institute
for Public Policy Research

1
Introduction

This monograph contains two distinct but related studies, and this introduction serves to make the link between the parts more transparent. The volume deals with both basic principles and practical options for agricultural commodity policy. It comprises two of eight major research studies on agricultural policy that were invited by the American Enterprise Institute for Public Policy Research.

AEI has a long tradition of sponsoring studies that have tried to bring economic analysis and common sense to the debate on agricultural policy in the United States. Early in 1993 AEI began to consider how best to make a contribution to what was likely to be an interesting opportunity for real progress in reforming the government's role in agriculture. AEI decided to sponsor several research studies that would each examine a part of the agricultural policy landscape with an eye toward a thorough reevaluation of "The Governing of Agriculture," a topic Bruce Gardner had examined in his 1981 book, *The Governing of Agriculture*. The results of the research are now being published as a series of monographs with short versions of each study in the volume *Agricultural Policy Reform in the United States*, which I have edited for the series.

Brian D. Wright and Bruce L. Gardner were both involved in previous AEI farm policy projects and were obvious scholars to draw on again in 1995. Wright is a leading academic researcher on agricultural issues and is an expert in commodity storage among other topics. As an Australian teaching in California, Wright brings an international perspective to considering the foundations of American agricultural policy. Gardner has both academic and practical credentials. He directed a previous AEI agricultural policy project and is the author of a number of influential books and academic articles on the economics of agriculture. In the 1970s Gardner served at the President's Council of Economic Advisers. More recently, he was assistant secretary of agriculture for economics and helped create some of the more market-oriented features of the 1990 farm legislation.

In the first part of this volume, Brian Wright considers the fundamentals of agricultural policy. He was asked to examine potential policy options without being constrained to what was likely to be politically popular. As he phrases it, he examined what agricultural policies the U.S. government should write on a clean slate. Wright begins by examining reasons commonly offered to defend why the government intervenes in agriculture at all. The bulk of the essay is addressed toward clarifying the goals that move government to become involved—some would say "entangled"—in agriculture. He finds that most of the potential rationales used for farm programs are obsolete, infeasible, more appropriate for or more fully achievable by private efforts, or simply inappropriate as goals for public policy. Almost all current agricultural efforts of the federal government serve goals that are not supportable on objective grounds. Ultimately, Wright does see a useful limited role for government in assuring property rights, in research and information, and in a few other areas. His major thrust, however, is that most of farm policy in the United States should be either removed by the roots or at least pruned severely.

The second part of this volume was designed to be more moderate and perhaps more practical in the short run. The assignment that Bruce Gardner accepted was in some ways less fun for an ivory tower economist than examining policy fundamentals. But his topic, to consider practical short-term policy adjustments, was also at least as challenging. Building on his experience as a close observer of and participant in the reform of agricultural policy, Gardner was asked to examine policies as they currently operate and to provide analysis and suggestions that would move farm commodity programs in a positive direction. Focusing directly on the programs that form the heart of agricultural policy, Gardner examines present practice, recent reforms, and current proposals. He assesses pros and cons by using basic economic analysis and supply and demand models. He then proposes some concrete changes that allow for a stronger role for market realities while maintaining at least some of the present program structure. As was consistent with his assignment, Gardner did not describe his ideal for American farm policy. Instead, he proposed some innovative adjustments within a constrained set. His analysis and proposals, if followed, would move agriculture a long way along the path laid out by Wright in the first part of this volume.

Each part of this volume provides a useful contribution for the agricultural policy debate in 1995 and in the future. Together with the other volumes in this series, these studies are sure to help improve the debate. With some luck and some effort, they may also help improve public policy for agriculture in the United States.

DANIEL A. SUMNER
Frank H. Buck, Jr., Professor of Agricultural Economics
University of California, Davis

Agricultural Policy from the Ground Up: Goals for a New Regime

Brian D. Wright

2
Goals for a New Regime

People discussing agricultural policy can easily forget that *farm* and *problem* are two separate words. Farmers naturally emphasize the production and marketing problems that they can use to justify government assistance. Economists concentrate on problems with the agricultural policies themselves. They may thus forget that agriculture has been a great success story for consumers in this century. In the United States only 11 percent of income now goes to food, and only about one-third of that goes to farmers. The wheat in the Wheaties box costs less than the package. Essentially the entire population of the United States enjoys the privilege of a continuously adequate food supply.

The greatest rate of progress in U.S. agriculture, in terms of increases in productivity, has occurred since the Great Depression—the inception of pervasive government involvement in agriculture. That is no coincidence. Government policies played a key role in helping farmers emerge from the depression and in fostering the high rate of productivity growth ever since.

The sustained fast pace of growth of agriculture over the past sixty years had completely transformed its role as an employer and generator of income and product in the U.S. economy. Yet the broad goals of current American agricultural policy are essentially those embraced

I am grateful for the exceptional research assistance of Rachael Goodhue in preparing this study and for information and comments provided by Warren Johnston, Dan Sumner, Tim Wallace, and Marguerite Wright.

7

under the New Deal in the 1930s. Does this imply their enduring social justification, despite changed circumstances? Or is it inertia in analysis and in policy making that has kept those goals from reflecting the transformation of the agricultural sector?

The bulk of the quinquennial review of the farm bill, *The 1995 Farm Bill Policy Options and Consequences,* is quite reasonably oriented toward modifications of existing programs. Such modifications are, in the main, the most likely outcome of the farm bill, whether or not they are what economists would choose. We must hope that economic input can improve any program changes. By asking how we can make likely policy reform work better, economists have good prospects of making some marginal difference in the evolution of policy.

If, on the other hand, the 1995 farm bill ushers in a new policy era, economic analysis is potentially much more relevant for the bill. Policy revolutions are rare and highly unpredictable, but they can and do happen. The current farm bill review should address the opportunities that might arise if U.S. agricultural policy breaks the mold cast in the New Deal, a previous policy revolution. Economic analysis offers high potential returns in a wholesale policy reform. The availability of an anticipatory economic analysis for policy makers increases the likelihood that a new agricultural policy will be a better agricultural policy. Less optimistically, an economic analysis might offer a menu of long-run objectives for a process of gradual reform.

Accordingly, my task in this review is to address the question, What policies should the U.S. government write on a clean policy slate? I have the liberty of leaving pressing, relevant issues of modifications to current programs in other very competent hands.

Questions about the appropriate and feasible architecture of government agricultural policies would be easier to address in the absence of a history of intervention. Although continuity in administrative regimes is an important value, inertia or path-dependence is not a self-evident rationale for retaining a program designed six decades ago. The "zero option" deserves a place on the menu in any serious review. By considering the zero option and ignoring any constraints imposed by the nature of existing policies, I can discuss agricultural policy as it might be constructed from the ground up. Given the current state of the agricultural sector, what is the appropriate structure of a new agricultural policy?

In such a radical reassessment it makes sense to start with the ends rather than the means of agricultural policy. We should consider only policy goals that are currently feasible and relevant. This rule sounds elementary, but it is mostly honored in the breach.

Analysts of agricultural policy pay scant attention to identifying policy objectives and much less to assessing them critically. Economists criticize politicians for obfuscating objectives. But economists themselves obfuscate the analysis of existing agricultural programs when they look for a highly stylized policy objective to justify current programs or some variation of them. The demand for coherent economic models to evaluate marginal reform encourages that tendency. Like a contestant on *Jeopardy*, the economist produces a question to which price supports or crop insurance, to take two examples, is the answer. In discussing those examples, I shall show that economists fail to investigate whether farmers' actual needs for government intervention match the stylized objectives that policy models assume.

Here I focus my attention on the ends of policy. To organize the analysis, I place the actual or potential goals of U.S. agricultural policy in five classes. The first category comprises feasible, achieved, and now obsolete goals. The second class includes popular or desirable but infeasible goals. In contrast, the third category comprises popular, desirable goals that are efficiently achievable without public assistance. The fourth class includes relevant goals that are achievable only with public intervention but are inappropriate social objectives. The final category comprises feasible, relevant goals that are appropriate as social objectives.

Only the final class of goals can justify public agricultural policy measures. Distinctions between the fourth and final categories obviously incorporate strong normative judgments. But I believe the general classification of goals is otherwise relatively uncontroversial, given the available facts and a modest exposure to economic reasoning.

The advantage of organizing my economic analysis around goals is that I can eliminate policies motivated by goals in the first four categories from the new policy set without considering the means themselves in any detail. That I do in the next four chapters. In chapter 7 I recommend policy measures that might help satisfy feasible, relevant, and socially appropriate agricultural goals. Conclusions follow in chapter 8.

3
Feasible, Achieved, and Now Obsolete Goals

Truly successful social policies make themselves irrelevant. That has happened to the following venerable list of objectives, which comprises some of the greatest achievements of U.S. economic development.

Achieving Income Parity between Farmers and Nonfarmers

Persuasive evidence that U.S. agricultural policy has achieved income parity between farmers and nonfarmers is the complete elimination of any deficiency in the income of farm operator households. In 1990 the average income for farm operators was $39,007; the average income for all U.S. households was $1,600 less (Ray 1994, 6).

Policy makers might like to attribute that achievement to price supports and other policy-induced transfers. But some countries, in particular Australia and New Zealand, have achieved a similar income parity without large transfers per farmer from consumers or taxpayers. Indeed, those countries achieved income parity even as their own agricultural support measures were being dismantled and as they were simultaneously experiencing declining terms of trade in their major agricultural products. Eliminating the rural income gap signifies integration of the farm sector into the rest of the economy, not closer ties between farming and government.

11

Integrating the Farm Sector into the Modern Economy

U.S. Department of Agriculture figures indicate that the average farm household mentioned above received only $5,742 from farming in 1990 (Ray 1994, 6). Although there is some question as to the precision of farm income data, they correctly imply that the average farm family employs a large share of its resources off the farm. The family's returns to farm capital and labor are determined by what those inputs can receive in the much larger non-farm economy.

Historically, the dynamic equilibration of on-farm and off-farm incomes depended on migration off the land as farm productivity rose and prices declined (Kislev and Peterson 1982). Migration is now most important in the rural areas with low population density. That process is often misconstrued. Fisher et al. (1994, 2, emphasis added) note, for example:

> Income levels for many Great Plains counties are greater than or equal to the median for non-metropolitan counties. *However,* due to a lack of employment alternatives, this region is experiencing the highest rate of out migration of any rural region in the United States.

Although the connection may not be obvious to all observers, the high rate of migration from the region undoubtedly plays a key role in maintaining high incomes in the Great Plains. In areas with a larger nonfarm economy, rural infrastructure in the form of roads, transport facilities, and communications has rendered off-farm jobs widely compatible with on-farm residence. I anticipate that telecommuting technology, which can facilitate the performance of "off-farm" work within the farm residence, will enhance that integration.

Integrating farm families into the local nonfarm economy does not necessarily lead to farm prosperity. If barriers to migration isolate the local nonfarm labor force from the national economy, there might in fact be more local nonfarm jobs with low wages offered to residents with no option of selling their labor at a higher price elsewhere. Fisher et al. (1994, 2) indicate that farm families in the South face such a situation:

> The economy of the rural South is much more diversified than is found in the Great Plains. Much of the employment available to rural residents is low wage and low skill. Rural income levels in the South are the lowest in the country. More of the persistent poverty counties are in the South than in any other region of the United States.

Employment opportunities in the rural nonfarm sector do not mean that pockets of rural poverty, in which the farm and nonfarm economies are both regionally isolated from the economy at large, do not exist.

In coming years improvements in transport and communications that continue to eliminate barriers to migration, commuting, or telecommuting will very likely further alleviate the remaining problem of regional (rather than sectoral) income inequality. More of the remaining regional income inequality is then likely to be due to regional deficiencies in opportunities for education rather than for employment.

Providing Adequate Rural Credit for Agriculture

Farming is a highly capital-intensive business, and nearly three-quarters of that capital is in farm real estate. Access to land is the entry ticket to farm operation. The price of land and the conditions of credit supply set the terms for becoming a farm owner.

The price of land reflects expectations regarding the future stream of profits from farming and the long-term cost of capital. Thus, young farmers with little capital have difficulty acquiring land. When the outlook is for increasing profits (from either market forces or an increasing trend in price supports), the land price tends to be high relative to current profits. Therefore, debt service is a challenge in the early years, even if optimistic expectations are generally fulfilled (Melichar 1979). Similarly, an upward adjustment in land prices tends to offset the benefits of low or subsidized interest rates. If, on the other hand, current conditions are good but the outlook is bleak, land costs are lower—but so are the prospective rewards from farming.

Apart from long-term expectations about profits and interest cost, other determinants of the price and availability of land include transaction costs, inheritance laws, the tax treatment of capital gains, and the influence of inflation on the effective tax rate. Thus far, the complexity of the relationships has overwhelmed economists' capacity to model the determinants of the volume and timing of land turnover in agriculture, including the role of credit policy.

One does not need a full model to know that the total area farmed is virtually independent of agricultural credit policy. But credit policy can favor some groups relative to others in the competition for land and working capital. The Farmers Home Administration, for example, has as a matter of policy channeled its direct loans toward otherwise noncreditworthy farmers. Indeed, its history of high loan losses relative to other lenders attests to its success in identifying those who truly are unworthy of credit.

The origins of the Farmers Home Administration lie in the Great Depression of the 1930s, when there was a very natural concern with the operation of bank credit and other sources of finance for agriculture and for the economy as a whole. Since then, government has heavily intervened in farm lending. In the past decade the Farmers Home Administration has also functioned as a savior for other lending institutions by adopting their worst credit risks (Falk 1994). Thus, the agency's recent problems reflect the larger difficulties of the savings and loan industry in the 1980s, which themselves are largely the predictable result of offering depositors excessive public risk protection[1] that naturally encouraged banks to take excessive private risks (Wright 1993). It may also have encouraged very significant fraud (Akerlof and Romer 1993).

Given the recent history of the savings and loans, it is not comforting to observe that both formal and presumptive credit risk guarantees are the means used by the other major instruments of agricultural credit policy—the Farm Credit System and its independent entity, the Federal Agricultural Mortgage Corporation (Farmer Mac). The Farm Credit System operates as a borrower-controlled banking system with a market cost of capital reduced by its status as a government agency. Lenders apparently perceive its debts to be government-guaranteed. Since this guarantee is only implicit, however, it does not appear in accounts of anticipated government expense of the system, which is usually characterized as "private." Farmer Mac, which guarantees secondary market sales of real estate loans, also has the advantage of agency status. After serious solvency crises in the past decade, the main problem Farmer Mac faces seems to be low demand for its services. For the Farm Credit System, the major issue now seems to be vigorous competition from the private-sector banks, input suppliers, and other sources of credit that threaten to force the Farm Credit System to downsize (Boehlje, Duncan, and Lins 1994, 3).

Problems with private rural credit are now insignificant relative to the situation in the 1930s. The extent to which federally subsidized credit programs and guar-

---

1. Legally, deposits are insured 100 percent to $100,000 per account, but in practice liability is often virtually unlimited.

antees contributed positively to achieving the current level of competition is a topic beyond my mandate here. We have little reason to believe, however, that special-purpose banks for farmers are in any way essential today.

But old habits of thought die hard. Commentators such as Boehlje, Duncan, and Lins (1994, 12) still view as problematic the fact that an admittedly competitive lending market will prevent noncreditworthy individuals from entering farming:

> Continued contraction of the [Farmers Home Administration] program reduces the credit availability for those who are not deemed creditworthy by private sector capital markets, but it reduces government spending. With a smaller FMHA program, the ability to enter farming would become even more limited.

To the extent that cheap credit, like high product prices, tends to raise land values, it does not help new entrants. To the extent that it allows noncreditworthy entrants into farming, the initial cost of the credit subsidy is likely to be only the first chapter in a story with a sad ending for the entrants and the Treasury Department. The following recollection of Bob Bergland, former secretary of agriculture, regarding the effects of unrealistic price expectations, helps us anticipate the evolution of the plot:

> I met with a mostly younger set of growers who brought me their grievances. . . . The growers believed they had heard government officials say that the so-called "farm income problems" had been solved. . . . These younger people had bought or rented land during that [1973–1974] price run-up period, and by 1977 with the collapse of wheat prices, they had been left out to dry. Their plea was that I should raise price-support loan rates to a level of $5 a bushel so that they could service their land debt. That request reinforced what I had been told by an

economic mentor in Minnesota, Dr. Willard Cochrane, who argued that farm profits are always capitalized in land values (Browne et al. 1992, ix).

Encouraging nonviable farmers to buy land is likely in the long run to cost the taxpayer much more than the initial credit subsidy, and much of that cost is likely to be funneled through additional subsidized credit services.

Achieving an Orderly Transfer of Labor Resources from Agricultural to Nonagricultural Employment

In 1900 38 percent of the labor force was in agricultural employment and 44 percent of the population was rural. The figures are now less than 3 percent and about 26 percent, respectively. The years of huge rural-urban labor force flows, including the mass migrations of African Americans from the South, are long gone. Labor will continue to leave the farm sector, but there is no current evidence of serious disequilibrium in the labor market flows between agriculture and other sectors.

A novel phenomenon in recent decades is the extent to which farm households have become engaged in the nonfarm economy *while still living on the farm*, as noted above. The cost of migration no longer prevents farm residents from moving part or all of their family labor off the farm. In its place are the net costs of commuting, or, for the future, telecommuting, which have been reduced by public investments in roads and publicly and privately supported innovations in telecommunication and computation technologies.

Historically in the United States, as currently in many developing countries, the transfer of agricultural labor to manufacturing and services was an important determinant of the rate of development of the economy as a whole. In the 1990s the issue of labor transfer from agriculture as a contributor to total development is virtually irrelevant to the national growth process; the number of workers still potentially available annually for transfer is now a negligible portion of the labor force.

One or more of the above goals might still be relevant in other countries. But in the United States, policy makers should feel free to declare victory and move on to focus on other objectives.

4
Popular, Desirable, but Infeasible Goals

These goals tend to be standbys for political sloganeers, for whom they have two great attractions. They are inherently appealing to the electorate, and they can never be made obsolete by being fulfilled.

Making Farming Permanently More Attractive to the Young

Making farming permanently more attractive to the young by means of price supports, deficiency payments, or market quotas positively related to production capacity is a goal that appears to be embodied explicitly or implicitly in farm policies of most developed economies, and it is often part of the rhetoric in support of policy legislation. Regardless of the merits of the objective, it is not achievable by the means listed above. Nor are the means consistent with common notions of equity among farmers or in the economy as a whole. Such conclusions are not matters of opinion or expressions of value judgments; they are the implications of the workings of a competitive market economy.

In a competitive market, land rents adjust in response to changes in profits from farming. Once market participants recognize the prospect of future transfers that are related to farm size, land prices also increase. When there is a competitive market for land, farmers who own land when such policies become recognized have a capital gain. If, for example, the interest rate is 5 percent, a permanent policy that transfers $10 per acre per year to farmers causes a jump of $200 per acre in the land price—the value of a perpetuity of $10 per year. The fact that their land is worth more on the market does not make continuing to farm it any more or less attractive to landowners, except insofar as their increased wealth changes their attitude toward work.[1] New entrants to farming will find that the increase in the land price ($200 per acre) more or less offsets any anticipated future benefits from government transfers.

Agricultural economists as well as farmers are increasingly widely recognizing this capitalization effect. But many may not recognize that the scope of its implications is so wide as to render the goals of equalizing the distribution of income and of stabilizing farm income infeasible as well.

Equalizing the Distribution of Income by Measures Related to Landholdings

Currently, the major means of agricultural income redistribution include price supports, deficiency payments, or other measures whose value is related to landholdings. Assume for now that those measures change farmers' incomes in proportion to their effects on current farm receipts. Most of the program benefits go to a minority of large farms (Browne et al. 1992, 45). The families running these farms generally have incomes above the average for farm and for nonfarm families alike. Since removing all agricultural transfers would bring the income of the major recipients closer to the national nonfarm average, the goal of equalizing farm and nonfarm income does not justify current policies.

---

1. If it does, the effect is negative with respect to the goal under consideration if increased wealth encourages them to leave farming for an easier urban life.

Within farming, landholdings, output, and transfers to farmers are all highly skewed toward those with high income from farming.[2] A well-informed citizen can easily conclude that policies that increase farm revenues in proportion to landholdings or output are contrary to equity goals within the agricultural sector.

What is not so obvious is the fact that capitalization, discussed above, means that the inequity of transfers related to production applies only to the owners of farmland at the time when policy changes first become known to the market. Given competitive land markets, buyers of land after the policy change will pay the full capitalized value of the transfers. They do not gain significantly from the transfer program; the transfers are just about enough to pay for the increased cost of the land.

Even if the revenue flows are permanently skewed toward large farms, no significant inequity from a policy change persists to the next generation of farm families other than by way of effects on bequests from their forebears. Buyers of large farms have large, government-subsidized revenues because they are wealthy. They are not wealthy because their revenues were enhanced by policies in place when they bought their land.

Capitalization of transfers into the value of land (and other fixed assets) means that the widespread perception that policy skews wealth toward large landowning farmers is true only for those who are lucky enough to own land during unanticipated policy shifts. But capitalization also means that the gains of those particular landowners are huge relative to the effects on annual farm revenues. Permanent policy shifts have one-shot wealth effects, which farmers may or may not share with their heirs, who may or may not choose to be farmers.

---

2. Payment limitations are probably relatively ineffective owing to well-known loopholes.

Later entrants into farming and annual renters of land get no comparable benefits.

Thus, beside ensuring that policy cannot make farming attractive for all future generations, capitalization also means that policy changes induce large but barely perceived inequities among generations of farmers. The size of the intergenerational bias in favor of current as distinct from future landowners is, paradoxically, larger if the policies are perceived to be permanent than if they are seen to be temporary.

Stabilizing Farm Incomes

Assume, for now, that the means of stabilizing farm incomes are feasible. Assume also that farmers and potential entrants uniformly prefer stabilization. If all farmers find farms with more stable revenue streams more desirable, they will bid up the price of buying or renting such farms so that the anticipated advantages of stabilization are more or less completely offset by the higher value of land. Potential farm purchasers or renters who value stabilization more than others might be somewhat favored in the bidding process in that they pay a little less for stability than what it is worth to them. But their gain is only at the expense of their less risk-averse competitors in the land market.

If revenue support, input subsidies, or market stabilization increases market demand for the purchase or rental of farms, heavy additional intervention is needed for the government to keep the current landowners from reaping all the benefits as a one-shot wealth increase. The government can do that by expropriating land from its owners at prices that reflect values before the policy change. The government can then use nonmarket means, such as political preference or a lottery, to allocate that land to prospective purchasers or renters who pay below-market prices and receive a gain that would have

gone to the seller in a free market. In principle, the government could conduct this policy in a way that increases
equity between farmers, as in a successful land reform. I
doubt that many citizens believe that such intervention
should or would be part of U.S. agricultural policy at this
time.

Achieving Rural Development

The foundations of achieving rural development with
farm price supports and subsidies were laid in the Great
Depression, when the nonmetropolitan community was
principally a farming community. Now less than 10
percent of the nonmetropolitan labor force works in
farming. Most of the rest are nonfarm employees; services, manufacturing, and government all employ more
nonmetropolitan workers than the number in farming
(Browne et al. 1992, chap. 3). In the modern U.S. economy, policy makers cannot effectively foster rural development by setting agricultural price policies.

True, 516 nonmetropolitan counties were defined as
"agriculture-dependent" in 1986, but that classification
means only that more than 20 percent of the labor force
was in farming. Those counties had in total only 7 percent of the nonmetropolitan population (Browne et al.
1992, 25–27). To put that another way, 93 percent of the
nonmetropolitan population resides in counties that are
not by that definition dependent on agriculture. Assuming that agricultural policy could make farmers (already
a relatively high-income rural group) more prosperous,
how can we expect to tackle rural development in general by manipulating the welfare of a small, generally
relatively wealthy minority of the population?

For the minority of counties that are agriculture-
dependent, government agricultural policy could plausibly more significantly influence rural development. But
by what means? If a policy could encourage retention

23

of smaller, low-income farms, would that advance rural development? A series of studies by the Office of Technology Assessment in the mid-1980s (U.S. Congress 1986, 3–25; Swanson 1990, 29) found "mixed though weak" support in the Plains and South, and no support in the Midwest and Northeast, for the hypothesis that increased farm size harmed rural communities.

In the Plains, it is true, those studies found that decreased farm numbers reduced population and the number of retail stores. In such a sparsely populated area, with few alternative occupational choices, that is not surprising. As discussed earlier, the migration that closed the stores kept local rural incomes in those states above the national nonmetropolitan average.

The Office of Technology Assessment studies did find that industrial-type farming with large amounts of hired labor per farm—a tiny minority of all farms, but important in a few commodities in some regions—was associated with lower community well-being. There is a question of causality here, of course. Is the community poorer because such farms exist, or do such farms exist because the community is poor? Are migrant farm laborers in California poor because they work on California farms, or do they work on the farms because they are poor and that is their best option? To ask those questions is to answer them.

Indeed, to ask what agricultural policy can do for rural development is to get the big question backward. With most farm families earning most of their income off the farm and most the rural labor force employed in other sectors, the real issue is what rural development policy can do for farmers (Luloff and Swanson 1990). That question is outside the scope of this study, but I offer two thoughts. I know of no unequivocally successful agricultural policy targeted directly at rural development in any country. Rural development is and has long been claimed as an important goal in many countries, and it has been an important part of World Bank policy. Advocates of farm price policy as rural development policy should by now be able to point to some success stories, if such a strategy has any merit at all.

If rural development means rural but nonfarm "job creation" to maintain population numbers, that is beyond the scope of my mandate here. But I have a question. Is the South, a leader in rural job creation, a rural development leader? Or has rural job creation contributed to the South's lead in poverty-ridden rural counties by hindering the out-migration necessary to increase local equilibrium wages? Or did barriers to out-migration foster local rural employment? Those are complex questions; no doubt the answers are complex also.

Economic theory and empirical evidence do point to government's substantial role in developing agricultural and more generally rural communities. But government's role is providing public goods and related infrastructure, activities beyond the scope of what is normally called agricultural policy.

5
Popular, Desirable Goals That Are Efficiently Achievable Privately

Sociologists have identified folk myths that gain substantial credence in American culture. Alligators are breeding in urban sewers. Abductions are occurring regularly in suburban malls. Devil-worshippers are sacrificing scores of babies in the woods.

Saving Family Farming

Another pervasive folk myth in America is that family farming is fast disappearing, being swallowed up by impersonal corporations run by city dwellers or even worse, by foreigners. The true wonder is that this is almost completely untrue. Despite the industrial and post-industrial revolutions and the revolution in agricultural production technologies, the managerial structure of agriculture in the United States is typically a family with some part of a person-year of hired labor supplying a total of about one-and-one-half person-years per farm. Even more remarkable, those numbers have remained virtually unchanged for the whole of the past century.

Non-family-owned corporations operate less than one-third of 1 percent of U.S. farms, and foreigners own only 1.3 percent of all farmland (Browne et al. 1992, 46). Even of the largest farm size category, 89 percent is operated personally by their owners. Farmers do, of course, rent a great deal of land, although the numbers to some extent reflect accounting adjustments in response to government limitations on price support payments. But families who own much if not most of their land operate the vast majority of farms.

It is no coincidence that a family farm, with between one and two full-time adult workers or their equivalent, is the operational rule in countries without much agricultural policy intervention, like New Zealand, and others with totally different agricultural policies, endowments, and technologies, like India. The typical farm, spread over a significant amount of land and subject to unanticipated disturbances from weather, pests, and other aspects of the environment, places a premium on workers with intimate local knowledge who are sufficiently self-motivated and thus need no close supervision (Nerlove 1994). The farm family member fits such a job description.

A high degree of concentration of production under nonfamily corporate ownership exists only in certain highly specialized lines of business, usually with well-controlled, simple production processes and a need for highly coordinated processing and marketing of a perishable product, such as sugar in Hawaii and strawberries in California's Central Valley. Those exceptions should not obscure the rule that family farming remains the overwhelmingly dominant form of organization. On the other hand, family farms have a much more pervasive tendency to enter into product marketing and input purchase contracts with firms that supply feed and process the product (for example, broilers) or marketing cooperatives (for example, citrus fruits), but families own and operate those contracting farms. I shall discuss some aspects of that organizational trend below.

Like all myths, that of the disappearance of family farming has a grain of truth at its core. The number of family farms is continually falling, because almost all farms are family farms, and the total number of farms is falling. Indeed, over the past sixty years, the majority of family farms has disappeared, usually because the operator retires or dies without being replaced by an heir willing to and capable of taking over the farm. But family farmers still till the land and raise hogs and calves. As noted above, the typical size and organization of American farms, measured by the labor and managerial input, have remained astonishingly constant over much more than a century, a phenomenon seen in no other similarly significant private-sector productive activity. What has changed is that each farm family now works with much more land, and many "small farmers" are now mostly, in terms of labor allocation, not principally farmers at all.

Of course, we have no guarantee that family farming will forever be predominant. Technology for communication, supervision, and real-time access to advice and information systems by spatially dispersed workers is advancing very rapidly. Those technical changes may shift the nature of the typical operational structure in primary agriculture and replace family operation with some other dominant mode. In time, those developments may have large implications for agricultural policy.

On the other hand, the advantages of family operation may actually increase in the future. Most nonfamily operations specialize in a single commodity. Complex multiproduct farms seem to be especially suited to family operation. Family organizations may be particularly well equipped to respond to the complexities of complying with "green" regulations or of producing environmental amenities along with agricultural commodities. Environmental demands placed on farmers are bound to become more important in the years ahead.

Nor is it necessarily true that farm size, in terms of land area operated, will continually increase. As more stringent controls are placed on chemical inputs, for example, the demand for managerial skill and attention will probably intensify and increase the inherent managerial advantages of family operation, while perhaps reducing optimal farm size. Private demands for hunting and other environmental services from farmers may have a similar effect.

Recent evidence suggests that modifying farm policies can reduce farm size, but the means may be surprising. The one developed country that has sharply decreased the average farm size in the past decade did so not by increasing government intervention, but rather by deregulating (Sandrey and Reynolds 1990). In New Zealand the average farm size decreased from 277 hectares in 1984, when a policy revolution began, to 217 hectares in 1993, and the number of farms increased by 4 percent (Johnston and Frengley 1994, table 2). The number of full-time permanent employees also increased slightly.

New Zealand is the only example of a country that has almost completely dismantled a complex system of agricultural subsidies in the postwar period. The high unemployment in the nonagricultural economy may explain part of that phenomenon.[1] But observers also point to diversification of farmers into new products in the new free-market environment, including labor-intensive specialty horticulture, as well as conversion of formerly subsidized sheep farms to smaller dairy farms. Could it be that we would also see more farms in a free-market U.S. agricultural sector?

In a free market the evolution of demands, environmental constraints, and technology will jointly determine the optimal size and managerial structure of farms. Farm policy can reduce farms below that optimal size, if it is backed by the kind of coercive powers usually con-

---

1. U.S. history shows that a depression might increase the number of farmers.

sidered incompatible with democracy. Poland, for example, maintained a large number of very small, family-operated farms under a communist regime instead of encouraging the private sector to consolidate assets and become more productive. With current technology, no amount of coercion can produce an agricultural sector of peasant-sized, full-time family farms with operators earning incomes that are not peasant-sized but comparable to those of typical modern urban families. Those twin goals are incompatible: as a package, they belong in the "infeasible" category discussed above.

Providing Farm-Specific Consulting on Technical or Managerial Issues

In the United States the Cooperative Extension Service has historically offered farms free consulting service on technical or managerial issues. Recently, however, the trend has been to cede that service to private farm management consultants and input and equipment dealers.

In several countries the public sector now is increasingly working on a fee-for-service basis; the distinction between public and private is blurring. Where those services provide only private value for the client, a tendency toward privatization is probably desirable, depending on the relative efficiency of private versus public provision. If the service provides significant benefits that a fee-paying client would not capture, then public provision is indicated, as I further discuss below.

Supporting Applied Research on Fully Marketable Innovations

The production of new seed varieties for farmers' use is a relevant example of applied research aimed at fully marketable innovations as outputs. Historically, that has largely been a public-sector effort for products such as wheat. But the private sector is dominant in genetic innovation that can be protected against the unauthorized taking or reproduction of purchased seed.

This protection may be biological, as in hybrid corn, which enjoys genetic protection from reproduction and resale by farmers. Or government may provide protection by enforcing proprietary rights through the patent system and the protection of trade secrets. Expanded patent protection and improved technological means of identifying infringements have allowed the private sector to take over and indeed greatly expand the production of novel final genetic material for most varieties of plants. Having successfully developed the scientific foundations and also the appropriate legal protections, the government can now gracefully withdraw from much of the commercial seed production business.

6
Relevant, Socially Inappropriate Goals Achievable with Public Intervention

To this point my analysis has focused on prescreening goals of agricultural policy to eliminate those that are infeasible as objects of agricultural policy, obsolete in the United States, or achievable without public policy measures. Rejecting goals fitting the above categories is, I trust, relatively noncontroversial. Whether a given goal belongs in one or more of those categories is more debatable. The main issue, however, is recognizing the full implications of economics in competitive markets.

I now turn to consider relevant, plausibly feasible goals that require public intervention for their implementation. Intervention can be justified on two broad grounds. First, goals might involve distribution between individuals beyond voluntary transfers—redivision of the economic pie. Whether that redistribution is appropriate clearly depends on value judgments. Second, if some distortion of the private market induces it to fail to allocate resources efficiently, government policy might in principle at least partially remove the distortion—increase the size of the pie. Whether the size of the distortion to be removed outweighs the costs of government intervention is another question.

The goals now under consideration, having satisfied the screening criteria, are candidates for implementation by means of specific policies. Accordingly, I shall now focus on the means of implementation, where appropriate, in addition to the ends. In this chapter I consider objectives that, in my view, do not merit public pursuit at this time in the United States. I leave development of a menu of appropriate objectives to chapter 7.

Increasing Price Supports, Deficiency Payments, or Other Transfers to Make Current Farmers More Wealthy

The means of price supports, deficiency payments, or other transfers tied to land, quotas, or other assets with fixed supply comprise the major instruments of agricultural policy in the United States. There is a crucial distinction between the goal of making current farmers better off and the goal in chapter 4 of making farming permanently more attractive to the young. It is quite feasible for policy to make *current* farmers better off by unexpectedly *increasing* transfers to farmers. No matter whether the new flow of transfers is a once-for-all shift, a slow rise, or a temporary boost, the wealth increase is as abrupt and immediate as the spread of recognition of the implications of the policy change.

The more permanent that increase is perceived to be, the greater the immediate boost in landowners' wealth. Later entrants—as distinct from heirs or other beneficiaries of current farmers' transfers—do not benefit from the initial transfer increase, regardless of whether it was permanent. Those entrants benefit only from later unanticipated increases. Assuming that those do not eventuate, the latecomers must defend the current "permanent" transfers to protect the value of their existing holdings of land and any other farming-specific fixed assets. As time goes by, farmers sell their land and exit from farming. The majority of supporters of existing transfer policies changes from those who are trying to retain the benefits they received to those who never benefited in the first place. But the latter will desperately fight to protect themselves from policy reforms that would cause the value of their investments to fall.

The dilemma is that although transfers may inequitably benefit politically favored groups in the initial generation of beneficiaries, their subsequent removal is also inequitable; the cohort that owns the land when the agricultural price support policy is removed loses relative to its successors. A policy that benefits only one generation recruits defenders in all subsequent generations until the policy is repealed. Psychological experiments suggest that people will fight harder to prevent a loss than to achieve an equivalent gain. Does that help explain why today's agricultural policies look so much like those of the 1930s?

The situation of later entrants is analogous to the situation of subsequent older generations after the inception of a fixed, pay-as-you-go social security system in a country with constant population growth and fixed assets like land. Assuming no indirect effects on factor prices or interest rates,[1] the later old generations do not gain from social security; their benefits merely cover the accumulated cost of the contributions they made when they were young.

Taxpayers in my cohort might well wish that social security were not in place as an unfunded, pay-as-you-go scheme. But many of us would also be willing to fight to keep it in place in the next generation, so that we may recoup the cost of paying out our social security contributions. Similarly, when a farmer says that he does not want the farm bill to change policy very much but also admits that he would prefer a world with no price supports or subsidies, he is not being schizophrenic. The dead hand of the past forces him to support a policy structure he would never have chosen, were his asset values not dependent on its continuation.

---

1. Chamley and Wright (1987) consider the more general case.

Assuming that the type of inequitable redistribution just described is what is wanted, supports that are decoupled from the recipient's own production and investment decisions are, all else being equal, preferable to payments that vary directly with production. For a given set of beneficiaries, decoupling is efficient. It prevents the distributive aim from inducing distortions in the mix of inputs farmers choose. For example, price supports tend to encourage the substitution of other inputs, such as fertilizer, for land, while deficiency payments paid on a program yield per acre, independent of actual production, do not induce comparable distortions because the future program yield is not responsive to current output.

My own view of the type of redistribution just discussed is that it is generally undesirable. But in special circumstances, such as the Great Depression, perhaps it made sense to try to boost the fortunes of a particularly unlucky cohort of farmers, even at the expense of subsequent generations. A similar rationale could be offered for the initiation of pay-as-you go social security, also established during the Great Depression.

Transfers proportional to land or production are not egalitarian *within* the initial cohort—the cohort of true beneficiaries. That problem, in contrast to the intercohort inequity, is widely recognized. Agricultural payments of that general type currently predominate in the United States. A minority of larger farmers gets most of the benefits. Most farm program payments do not aid the poorest farm households, let alone the poorest rural households. Appalachia, the region with the lowest farm household incomes, received the lowest share of farm household income from government payments.

The skewed nature of the distribution of farm price supports among current farmers leads many commentators to advocate direct transfers to farm operators, independent of the assets they own or the size of their productive capacity. Would they be better?

Providing Egalitarian Direct Transfers to Farmers

From an equity standpoint, transfers totally independent of assets, output, and output capacity have two great advantages. First, they can be completely egalitarian within a cohort of farmers or even skewed toward those with lower incomes. Second, since they are not capitalized in fixed assets, they do not cause intercohort inequity by front-loading the discounted stream of benefits on the first cohort of recipients.

But payments to farmers *for being farmers* would be a disaster. What criteria would identify farmers? Rural lifestyle? Location on a farm? A certain percentage of time spent on agricultural labor?

Were any of the above criteria adopted, it is a good bet that the supply response of the number of farmers to a meaningful level of redistributive transfers would be impressive. That would in turn imply that a large proportion of recipients would not have been members of the originally targeted farm population. In addition, it would imply that the cost of the transfer per dollar to the originally targeted population could be correspondingly higher. Finally and most seriously, the beginnings of a permanent, unproductive class of government-dependent, rent-seeking peasantry would be created, with its members being diverted from more gainful occupations or more appropriate residential locations. The efficiency advantage of decoupled transfers is reversed if the set of farmer recipients responds to the transfers. For a current example of that type of problem, consult the recent history of Pacific islands that are "beneficiaries" of U.S. welfare programs. Whatever the shortcomings of U.S. agricultural policy, it has avoided that policy catastrophe.

Protecting Producers against Risk

The most pervasive rationale for interventionist agricultural policy in developed economies, and the one economists give the greatest respectability, is that farmers need government protection against risk to produce efficiently. That argument is distinct from its distributional counterpart, risk protection to make farmers better off, which is an infeasible long-run objective, as discussed above.

The efficiency argument for risk protection has great persuasive power. We all know that agriculture is subject to unusually large production disturbances, from weather fluctuations, pest infestations, and the like. Given the inelastic response of consumption to price that is typical of agricultural products, marketwide production disturbances translate into much greater price fluctuations. Since agricultural production takes time, the farmer has to make financial commitments to input choices for crop or animal production well before he knows output prices and yields. The result is that net income from most agricultural production activities is highly risky. Can government make farmers more efficient on average by reducing their reluctance to take production risks?

Private insurance usually is not available to remove all income risk and in many cases is not offered at all. Its absence lends credibility to the economic case for public intervention to create this "missing market" and ease the "capital rationing" that arises because of risk aversion.

Variants of the above argument are the main intellectual defense of major existing U.S. agricultural policies, including price floors, nonrecourse loans, deficiency payments, crop insurance, and marketing orders. The recent Iowa Farm Bill Study Team's plan (1994) and other revenue insurance proposals appeal to that rationale.

Economists realize that most of the above programs tend to raise incomes rather than to stabilize them. But economists continue to give the risk-reduction argument inordinate weight by using an analytical approach that greatly overstates the value to farmers of policies reducing the risk of their income flows from farming.

Economists generally use expected utility theory,

the dominant approach to the economics of risk, in policy analysis of risk-taking, market stabilization, and insurance. Utility is a function of consumption. But agriculturally oriented studies tend to model utility as a function of income. They assume that a farmer's consumption tracks his farm income, which means that consumption fluctuates just as wildly as farm income. All private means of smoothing the effects of farm income on consumption are ignored.

Accordingly, economists overestimate the risk premium, a measure of the gain from smoothing consumption around a given mean. The risk premium increases roughly proportionally to the variance in consumption. So if the farmer smoothed half of each deviation in net income relative to the mean income, the remaining cost of risk would be only one-quarter of the unsmoothed value that the economist assumed.

In fact, without any special government intervention, farmers are extremely capable of smoothing their consumption flows relative to their unusually variable farm income stream. The methods they use include diversification of income sources, saving, and borrowing. Since analysts frequently ignore those methods, they bear some elaboration.

Diversifying across Space. By incorporating fields with different soil types, farming bottom land and hillsides, or even exploiting local differences in rainfall patterns or soil water-holding capacity, a farmer can in many cases very considerably reduce exposure to weather-related risk.

Single-field observations of risk can greatly overestimate the farm-level cost of risk. For example, in the Experiment Station of the International Crops Research Institute for the Semi-Arid Tropics in a semiarid area of India, correlation of July rainfall between two ends of the 1,400-hectare station is only around .6 (Walker and Jodha 1986, 25). Diversification of a peasant's small plots within the area around a local village can obviously reduce yield variation substantially (McCloskey 1976).

Diversifying across Activities. Diversification might come in the form of a mix of crops such as corn and soybeans. Diversification across crops and livestock, as in corn-hog or corn-beef operations, is a natural way of combining activities with countervailing sensitivities to the vagaries of the animal feed market; when the price of corn is low, meat production is cheaper, and vice versa. But even if two activities have unrelated, rather than off-setting, sources of income fluctuations, a great consumption-smoothing advantage lies in diversifying across the two, rather than in specializing. If both activities have equal mean and variance of incomes, farmers can reduce the cost of consumption fluctuations in terms of risk premium by one-half by giving each an equal share in the farm operation, rather than specializing in one or the other.

Diversifying into Off-Farm Employment. The above on-farm diversification strategies are most pertinent for the minority of farm families that specializes in farming. But most U.S. farmers, as noted above, receive much more of their income from off-farm employment than from farming. We know that most farmers live in counties where most of the income is not related to agriculture. Unless off-farm income is highly correlated with the farmer's on-farm income, this diversification will very substantially dampen the general relative variability of the farmer's consumption. If, as is likely, off-farm income is steadier than on-farm income, and the two are approximately independent, then most of the risk cost of farm income fluctuations would be diversified away for the typical farmer merely by means of off-farm employment. To take a simple example, a farmer with one-third of family income from a certain type of farming would obtain only about one-ninth the benefit from complete stabilization of farm income, relative to another farmer with the same mean income who was totally specialized in the same type of farming.

Adjusting Savings and Borrowing. Another extremely important means of consumption smoothing is adjusting savings or borrowing. Even in developing countries with neither the diverse financial markets seen in the United States, nor the off-farm income diversification, nor the extensive agricultural price supports, it appears that savings or formal or informal loans buffer much if not all of farmers' short-run income shocks (Paxson 1992; Alderman and Paxson 1992).

A tough test of farm families' ability to handle shocks is the extent to which severe fluctuations in income associated with an abrupt cutoff of large agricultural subsidies translates into movements in consumption. The recent experience of New Zealand provides an example. In 1984 the newly elected labor government of New Zealand abruptly reformed economic policy by placing it on a free-market path. The agricultural sector experienced the rapid dismantling of a system of large subsidies on products and inputs including fertilizer and capital. In addition, the government sold the rural bank to the private sector. Agriculture was also affected by tariff reductions, an abrupt devaluation and subsequent revaluation of the currency, and a rapid escalation in interest rates. Total measured government assistance of all kinds, including infrastructure, plummeted between 1984 and 1986, except that debt forgiveness continued to be important for a few more years. The producer subsidy equivalent—an indicator of government protection measured as a percentage subsidy on production—for sheepmeat, a historically important export, declined from an average of around 60 percent in the first half of the 1980s to 13 percent in 1986 and continued to decline; the producer subsidy equivalent for beef fell from 20 to 10 percent (Webb, Lopez, and Penn 1990, 196, 199).

Figure 6–1 shows the effects of that experience on a

FIGURE 6–1

NEW ZEALAND SHEEP AND BEEF FARMERS' USE OF SAVINGS AND
BORROWING TO SMOOTH CONSUMPTION, 1983–1992

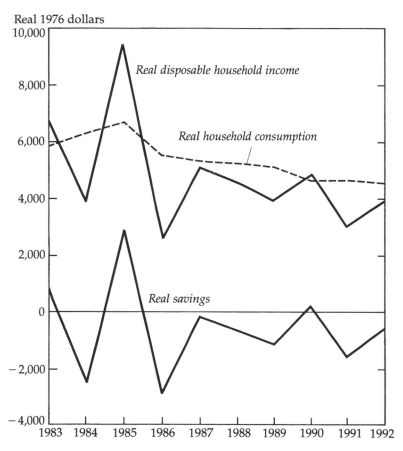

SOURCES: Frengley and Johnston (1992, table 2), Johnston and Frengley (1994, table 6), and unpublished data from New Zealand Meat and Wood Board's Economic Service.

measure of disposable income of the average beef-sheep farmer. Real disposable income fluctuated wildly, but adjustments in saving or changes in debt buffered most of the year-to-year variation. Consumption remained remarkably steady. One would naturally expect that high-

FIGURE 6–2
Highly Indebted New Zealand Sheep and Beef Farmers' Use of Savings and Borrowing to Smooth Consumption, 1985–1992

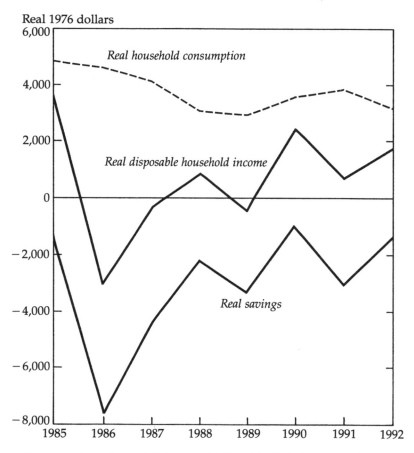

Sources: Frengley and Johnston (1992, table 3), Johnston and Frengley (1994, table 6), and unpublished data from New Zealand Meat and Wood Board's Economic Service.

debt farms would have the least flexibility for that type of adjustment. In figure 6–2 I show the experience of those farms since 1985. It is not surprising that those farms have somewhat lower real consumption. What is striking is that in the sample, chosen each year for its high degree of leverage, and thus most likely to be credit-rationed, real consumption is relatively insensitive to fluctuations in disposable income because it is buffered by changes in net debt.

I use foreign sources for my empirical analysis of risk management because analysts have collected little empirical evidence in the United States regarding either the economic need for protecting farmers' risk or the risk-protection value of current or proposed policies. This is so despite the prominence of risk reduction in the deductive arguments and theoretical analysis supporting U.S. policies and despite the large expenditures at stake. Farmers might not want the question of risk reduction scrutinized, if they suspect, based on their own experience, that the answer would not help the case for the policies they want. But why has the agricultural economics profession been so incurious about the empirical validity of its theories?

If the appropriate empirical work were done, I believe it would not support the risk-protection argument for agricultural policy. The best U.S. evidence I know on the response of farmers' consumption to income fluctuations is data on eighteen Illinois farmers from 1979 through 1986 that Langemeier and Patrick (1990) analyzed. Using various conventional models, they find a marginal propensity to consume out of current income of less than .03: a dollar of income fluctuation translates into a change in consumption of less than three cents.

Although the models used are subject to theoretical challenges, figure 6–3 tells the main story. In a period of wild fluctuations in family income—as well as in interest rates, credit availability, and net worth—consumption is remarkably steady relative to income.[2] Note that those income fluctuations constitute the variation that remains *after* the stabilizing effects of commodity policies such as target prices, nonrecourse loans, and crop insurance.

---

2. Its standard deviation is only one-tenth that of income in the sample.

FIGURE 6–3
INCOME AND CONSUMPTION OF EIGHTEEN ILLINOIS FARM FAMILIES, 1979–1986

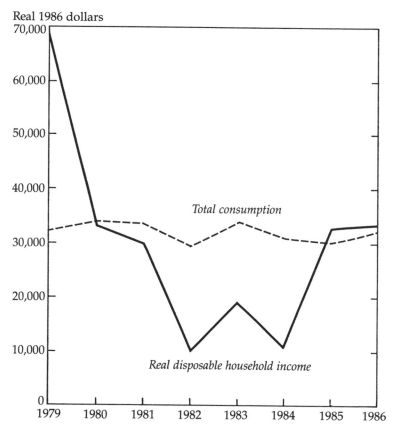

SOURCE: Langemeier and Patrick (1990, table 1).

Clearly, those programs do not achieve a smooth income stream for farmers, but farm families nevertheless quite successfully smooth consumption.[3] Those figures establish that any analysis that assumes that income equals

---

3. Consumption may reflect the stabilizing effects of access to publicly provided or guaranteed loans.

consumption, year by year, is radically misspecified and will vastly overestimate the effect of policies designed to reduce risk.

Farmers' Responses to Expanded Alternatives for Reducing Risk. Thus far, my discussion of risk has centered on farmers' alternatives for risk management and evidence about their aggregate efficacy. But if those alternatives, although effective, were sufficiently costly, farmers would welcome opportunities to smooth consumption by adopting measures that stabilize their incomes and make their production plans more predictable. One way to explore this possibility is to observe farmers' choices when presented with opportunities to reduce risk. The available evidence is instructive.

Crop insurance worldwide. As described elsewhere (Hazell, Pomareda, and Valdés 1986; Goodwin and Smith 1995; Wright and Hewitt, 1994), of the many crop insurance schemes governments in developing and developed countries have tried over many years, none has attracted the participation of the majority of farmers without a substantial government subsidy. A common-sense conclusion is that farmers do not have a high enough risk premium to make participation on an actuarially fair basis covering reasonable administrative costs sufficiently attractive, given their other alternatives for smoothing consumption.

An alternative interpretation is more popular with economists, who are attracted by its more interesting theoretical content and its consistency with the general economics literature on insurance. In that rationale the problem is that the government as insurer cannot observe the true insurability of a given farmer and his actions relevant to risky outcomes. Thus, unusually risky farms will be most likely to apply for insurance; economists call this adverse selection. In addition, insured farmers will tend to be less careful to contain risks; they may even cheat. Economists call those possibilities moral hazard. To cover the increased risk of loss, premiums must be higher. But higher premiums tend to discourage the less risky farmers from buying insurance and thus exacerbate the problem of adverse selection. The upshot is that the expected losses of the insured might be so high that a private insurer could not make a profit from that type of insurance, even though farmers are quite averse to risk.

Were an insurance contract developed with payouts highly correlated with crop income, but independent of the type of farmers who apply and how they behave, then moral hazard and adverse selection should be irrelevant. If farmers had a large demand for crop insurance that is unmet because of moral hazard, adverse selection, or both, the insurance just described should find a ready market. Does it? The next example provides a test.

Rainfall insurance. In the high-risk, low-rainfall Mallee wheat-growing area of Australia, the government took the unusually sensible step of asking farmers whether they would be willing to buy insurance before implementing an insurance program.[4] The proposed contract had payouts conditioned on local rainfall measurements, and the price was actuarially fair and covered standard administrative costs. Note that such insurance avoids the usual problem of moral hazard and adverse selection, since producers cannot, by their decisions on participation or crop management, influence the local rainfall risk faced by the insurer.[5]

---

4. Governments usually try crop insurance programs that end up losing millions if not billions of dollars without ever seriously considering research to see whether the program is needed or why it is not working. Despite the billions of dollars lost on those programs every year, I know of no research in any country that examines the influence of crop insurance on farmers' consumption patterns.

5. Some farmers did worry that the rainfall readings might be manipulated by the insurer, but pains were taken in the course of the survey to reassure farmers on that point.

Farmers indicated rainfall as their number-one farm risk. They were not averse to insurance in general; the vast majority of the sample had above-minimum levels of life and automobile insurance. But the majority did not wish to purchase rainfall insurance. That survey evidence supports the simple hypothesis advanced above, that crop insurance is a money-losing proposition because it is simply of insufficient value to farmers.

Some economists have offered an alternative hypothesis: The rainfall insurance was not popular because what farmers want is revenue insurance, not output insurance. In the case of Australian wheat farmers, that alternative is unappealing because price risk is less important than output risk, and the two are not mutually offsetting. But from Canada we have more direct evidence of farmers' preference for revenue insurance versus output insurance.

Revenue insurance. In Saskatchewan, Canada, the federal and provincial governments jointly implemented the Government Revenue Insurance Program in 1991 as comprehensive insurance against income risk due to fluctuations in price or yield. If farmers are risk averse according to the standard theoretical model of insurance, they should prefer income insurance to price or yield insurance.

Saskatchewan farmers did not behave in accordance with that model. They successfully lobbied for a separation of the price and yield insurance aspects the following year, apparently on the grounds that they preferred payouts on price shortfalls, even if income were unusually high, given large yields, and vice versa. Although there are undoubtedly other considerations at work in this case, the farmers' behavior does not seem to provide evidence of the conventional risk aversion argument for crop insurance. But their behavior is consistent with the hypothesis that they are not sufficiently risk averse to value crop insurance highly.

Production contracts. In the United States comprehensive production contracts have been spreading from products like broilers and processed vegetables into other product lines including pork production. Those contracts generally fix input and output prices and offer various degrees of access to technical assistance. Apart from any concerns about monopsony or monopoly, farmers frequently object to those contracts because they do not allow contract farmers to participate in price increases. Farmers usually ignore the fact that the contract equally protects against price decreases. The farmers' objection would be consistent with the standard risk aversion model if their output were inversely proportional to price. Then price stabilization on its own could destabilize income. In industries with highly controlled environments, it appears unlikely that yield movements of the typical contractor would counterbalance the effects of price movements on income. It appears, then, that contractors who make that complaint actually prefer price risk.

That should not be very surprising. If producers can respond to price variations and their yield disturbances are small or independent of prices, their average profits are higher when their input and output prices are variable than when they are stable at their mean values. Preference for nonstabilized prices over contractually fixed prices indicates that risk aversion is not the dominant determinant of those producers' attitudes toward price stabilization by private contract. Why would they favor similar stabilization by the government in the absence of a sweetener in the form of a rise in mean price?

7
Policies to Write on a Clean Slate

In general, government interventions to improve efficiency come under the headings of either providing public goods or of correcting externalities and other market failures. Public goods are goods or services that the private sector cannot provide efficiently. If supplied to one person, they are available to others at no extra cost. Thus, one person's consumption does not reduce the availability of public goods to other people. Since the good is available to nonpaying consumers, producers are not able to charge a positive price. And even if such a "free riding" can be prevented, the policy of charging each consumer the marginal cost of consumption, while generally efficient in covering costs for private goods, fails for public goods. Marginal cost, the cost of providing another unit of (joint) consumption, is less than the average cost of production, so to price at marginal cost is to run a deficit. Moreover, it is economically undesirable to enforce a higher payment by the marginal consumer, because to do so is to prevent some consumption that is more valuable to consumers than what it cost to produce the good. Those characteristics are obvious in the "pure" example of radio market reports or a new production technique, where the cost of one more farmer's acquiring the use is zero and it is not possible to charge a fee. Less pure cases might still merit public provision if the private alternative is less efficient.

An externality is a related phenomenon wherein one

party's production or consumption activity affects the profits or utility of another in the absence of any market transaction between the two. The examples of the positive interaction between beekeeping and clover production and the negative example of environmental pollution are typical. Other types of market failure include cases in which a market for a good or service is distorted, as in conventional (nondiscriminatory) monopoly, or is missing altogether.

Recent econometric analysis of the agricultural sector in developing countries suggests that, while agricultural supply generally responds to price incentives, the provision of certain types of public goods can be much more important for the growth of agriculture. Among those are roads, communication systems, health services, and general education, all of which are already available in the United States and hardly come within the range of what is called agricultural policy in this country. Others are crucial elements of U.S. agricultural policy, including agricultural research, environmental services, domestic food assistance, and food security.

Conducting Agricultural Research to Produce Externalities

From a large number of studies in many countries, economists have reached an all-too-rare consensus that public agricultural research is a highly productive public investment, with rates of return that are exceptional by any standard. Although research results are often transferable across regions or countries, local research is usually needed for successful adaptation to local conditions.[1] Countries or regions that attempt to take a free ride on research tend to get left at the starting gate.

In the United States the history of increasing yields

---

1. This is especially true for crops but is less true for animal production (Huffman and Evenson 1993).

and sustained productivity growth matches, with perhaps a thirty-year lag, the period of heavy public involvement in the agricultural sciences. If there was ever a truly successful "industrial" policy, it is U.S. agricultural research policy.

The agriculture-related sciences, in particular the biological sciences, are changing with the revolution in genetic engineering. In many disciplines the path from the basic science to the usable agricultural innovation appears to be shortening, and traditional product-related specialization is becoming obsolete. One of my colleagues is a scientist who has been involved in the breeding of bacteria that can protect strawberry leaves from frost and of a close relative that can be used to make snow on ski slopes. I doubt that he would appreciate it if his job description restricted him to working on strawberries alone.

Paradoxically, at a time when Washington would love to find a vehicle for applying industrial policy, it is cutting back on support for the only industrial policy with a worldwide, sixty-year record of great success. And just when applied researchers need to be closer than ever to their mother academic discipline, the tendency nationwide has been toward funding special-purpose applied research centers concentrated on a particular crop or issue.

That problem is not restricted to the federal administration. At the University of California, the agricultural vice-president has decided to transfer funds from more basic agricultural science at Berkeley to the applied, product-constrained fields at other campuses, just as those fields are tending toward obsolescence or are being taken over by the private sector.

Modern public agricultural research should build on its history of success by emphasizing close links with the rapidly advancing mother disciplines. That research should be sufficiently flexible to take advantage of op-

51

portunities for applications as and where they arise.[2] With recent expansion in the patenting of life forms, stronger patent enforcement by courts, and the more effective policing afforded by genetic fingerprinting technology, the private sector is taking up more of the final developmental research. The government can withdraw some resources from that developmental work and reallocate them to the more basic agricultural sciences to enable the agricultural sector to provide modern environmental and ecological services to society at large.

The current widespread concern about lack of direction in agricultural research partly reflects the destabilizing effects of the challenges posed by the new biotechnology and other modern approaches. But agricultural economists have also pointed out that in a distorted economy "successful" innovations can be less socially beneficial or can even reduce social welfare, because they increase the wasteful misallocation of productive resources induced by the policy structure. It does not take an economist to recognize that increasing the production of surplus commodities is undesirable. In an agricultural sector that starts with a clean policy slate, as considered here, that problem would disappear.

Providing Environmental Services
Not Privately Capturable

Concern with environmental degradation in agriculture existed at the beginnings of current agricultural policy in the depression years of the Dust Bowl. Until recently, the major concern has been the correction of externalities acting *within* agriculture. Control of wind and water erosion protected productive topsoil. A related concern was protection of water storage from silting, a concern at least partly directed to the maintenance of irrigation

---

2. For more on research administration, see Just and Huffman (1992).

facilities. Thus, conservation has meant conservation *for* agriculture *by* agriculture. But it seems that the Dust Bowl was in large measure the result of short-term ignorance of nature by relatively recent settlers; it points to the need for timely public information more than to the need for regulation. Properly informed farmers who have secure tenure are generally careful to prevent the wholesale migration of topsoil that was seen in the 1930s.

Now, however, society is becoming increasingly aware of the off-farm environmental consequences of farming, including not just erosion but also water pollution, flooding, air pollution, and the release of toxic or ozone-depleting substances. Furthermore, farmers are increasingly being asked to play host to predators they had previously eradicated from their localities, such as wolves, coyotes, or mountain lions, and to previously insignificant animals now decorated with the title "endangered." Farmers are being pressured to meet new standards of respect for animal rights, often by people with questionable familiarity with the habits or needs of the animals in question. In short, the public is starting to demand that farmers produce not merely food and fiber, but also a host of environmental amenities, some more quantifiable than others.

We cannot now know how those demands will play out. Although environmental groups' current attitudes toward price support policy versus free markets seem rather confused, as time goes by a consensus should develop against incentives that increase the intensity of use of chemical inputs. Societies with the highest farm price supports—including Japan, South Korea, and the European Union—have the highest levels of input use. Within the latter, the Netherlands is already taxing fertilizer use as an environmental policy.

The experience of New Zealand confirms the positive relationship between protection and chemical inputs. Removal of subsidies on farm inputs and outputs in New Zealand resulted in a fall of 55 percent in fertilizer use by agriculture between 1980 and 1986. While that initial fall overstates the long-run adjustment in fertilizer use, total farmland area also declined, despite the fact that farm numbers increased.

It is instructive to compare the reform-induced decline of 18.4 percent in New Zealand farmland from 1984 through 1993 (Johnston and Frengley 1994, table 2) with the approximately 8 percent of U.S. cropland—3 percent of total agricultural use or 36.5 million acres—enrolled in the Conservation Reserve Program in 1993 (U.S. General Accounting Office 1993). Note that the idled New Zealand land, which includes abandoned high-country pastoral properties, is not subject to conservation requirements like those of the U.S. Conservation Reserve Program. But a significant amount of land is being converted to forestry, a trend encouraged by eliminating subsidies on competition from public forests. Forestry is a more permanent conserving use than the Conservation Reserve generally achieves.

Environmental policy has already reached beyond adjustments in conventional farm policy. Current attempts to extract services by using coercive regulation to "take" profits are likely to fail. Experience with species such as the black-footed ferret suggests what should be quite obvious. To demand that any farmer who finds a black-footed ferret on his property obey expensive constraints on the operation of the farm is to ensure that no farmer will report ferrets, and the chance that visitors will get to see any is likely to be slim. On the other hand, bounties to farmers for high counts of live endangered species could have a totally different effect on their numbers.

It is clear that agricultural policy governing environmental issues will move well beyond the existing Conservation Reserve Program in the future. We can expect policy to be more accurately targeted toward environmental goals, as distinct from reducing farm output. Achieving a multiplicity of environmental goals through agricultural policy is likely to be a daunting task. Markets work best when outputs are standardized products sold in a competitive setting. Traditional agricultural products generally fit such a description. Environmental outputs, on the other hand, are generally multiple joint products, often more qualitative than quantitative, of agricultural production. The challenge is to design policies that include an incentive structure that preserves the remarkable benefits of an efficiently decentralized farming system while satisfying those new demands.

Assisting Disadvantaged Consumers

I am reluctant to include food stamps in my list of "clean slate" policies. In the absence of historical precedent and political logrolling, it is dubious whether food stamps, the Special Supplemental Program for Women, Infants, and Children (WIC), subsidized school lunches, and similar measures would be classified as agricultural policies at all. But as it is, their cost of $34 billion (Kinsey and Ranney 1994, 1) constitutes a major part of agricultural expenditures, more than the federal cost of all farm programs.

From the farmer's viewpoint, the crucial question is whether those programs increase the demand for farm products in excess of what an equivalent income transfer would achieve. The conventional response is "not by much." On the other hand, the reported market price discount of fifty cents on the dollar for food stamps suggests that they are not just treated as extra income, as many economists assume. I understand that analysis of the WIC program shows great cost effectiveness by way of a reduction in later social expenditures for the mother and child. A crucial issue is whether and how those in-kind transfers affect the distribution of access to resources among family members. Different models suggest different outcomes. It would be interesting to know whether the means of transfer (stamps versus school lunches versus money) can increase the welfare of the more disadvantaged members of households by changing their bargaining power, especially in the chaotic environments often seen in the poorest families.

A downside of transfer programs like food stamps is that they can also be viewed as programs that increase the already high tax rate on poor people struggling to escape poverty. On the other hand, that is a characteristic of any program targeted at the currently poor. If society continues to support transfers of current magnitudes to the poor, food stamps and particularly the WIC program are good means of making the transfer.

Providing Food Security

The past several decades have been an era of remarkably stable, steadily increasing worldwide food production. Although there are regional harvest failures every year, they have not of themselves caused famines. The localized famines that have occurred have been attributable to political factors and interference with trade and distribution of aid, usually in association with a military conflict. For local disturbances in output, governments' commitment to open trade and humanitarian emergency aid is an adequate guarantee of food security. For the much less probable significant global shortages, the solution is less simple.

In the United States and indeed the entire Western world, the vast majority of the current population has never experienced a serious interruption of its food supply. Nevertheless, food security should remain an important objective of agricultural policy. We cannot be sure that the world's food supply in the next generation will be as stable as it has been for the previous generation.

We cannot expect the private sector to provide adequate protection against shortages. Experience has shown that there is a substantial probability that contracts that guarantee resource supply might be effectively repudiated when prices rise unexpectedly.[3] Even if this were not true, anticipated government actions in an emergency dampen the incentive to provide private emergency supplies. Experience in the energy crises of the 1970s indicates that in a commodity shortage the government will interfere with private storage, pricing, and trade to prevent hoarding and price-gouging. Sometimes those measures are made explicit in advance. California has recently prohibited a markup of over 10 percent for supplies provided after an earthquake to prevent the exploitation of consumers.

Presumably, California does not wish to impose an ex ante disincentive for the private sector to provide food security. But the state is probably incapable of committing itself to refrain from interfering with profits from emergency supplies ex post. Unfortunately, such a market failure is self-reinforcing; given a level of disincentive, the private sector reduces its emergency supply capacity, which makes the shortage and the equilibrium "price-gouging" more likely. That only increases the expectation that the government will limit the profitability of private emergency supplies ex post (Wright 1992).

Given the constraints on private-sector incentives, what is the appropriate public food security policy? That question is difficult to answer, in part because it depends on the probability distribution function of world food harvests. We have enough data on the latter to have some confidence that the past few decades have furnished an unusually stable food supply, but we have too small a sample of observations to be very sure about the fre-

---

3. Consider, for example, the case of the Westinghouse guarantee to supply uranium to purchasers of its reactors in 1981.

quency of global shortages of various degrees of severity. For a precise calculation of the probability of relatively infrequent events such as serious harvest failures, we require a very large number of harvest observations, even if the general environment is not changing over time.

Another problem that we should address is the possibility of disruption of the domestic food supply system after the harvest. The same functional and regional specialization that improves productivity also tends to make the population more susceptible to interruptions in domestic flows of food by wars, terrorism, sabotage, and earthquakes or other large-scale natural disasters. Perhaps the current structure of the food supply system ensures that a large-scale disruption of the food supply is virtually impossible. But has the Office of Emergency Preparedness or any other agency made a serious study of that issue? Or are we waiting for a real-world experiment?

It is instructive to remember that until the great blackout of 1965 in the Northeast, electric utilities and consumers assumed that such a widespread interruption of the supply network could not result from localized damage to transmission facilities. The possible short-run disruption of food distribution within the specialized economy of the United States may or may not be a problem; surely it deserves at least a modicum of research attention to decide whether it is.

For the longer-term problem of a possible shortfall in the global food harvest due, for example, to a multi-year drought in an important producing region, parts of an acreage reserve, perhaps the successor to the current Conservation Reserve, could furnish relatively low-cost reserve productive capacity to respond, with about a year's lag, to the crisis. Public or private stocks held in different countries could furnish a more immediate response. The arrangements of the International Energy Agency for international coordination of supplies from stocks in a petroleum supply emergency might be a useful first reference for a study of food supply arrangements in a global food emergency.

Protecting against Monopoly or Monopsony

Individual producers of most agricultural commodities are numerous and competitive; they have no ability to control the prices of their inputs and outputs. Economies of large size are much more significant in the industries that provide inputs and process and market agricultural outputs. For commodities with large transport costs, a farmer might have only one or two feasible input suppliers or output purchasers. In such a situation, farmers—especially those who must make long-term commitments to crop-specific investments, as in the case of tree crops or dairies—cannot ignore the possibility that their market might be distorted by the exercise of market power on the input or output side.

It might be impossible for a dominant processor of a commodity credibly to promise not to exploit his potential suppliers. A pear canner might promise a high price to pear growers until they have planted their trees. But he will be tempted to lower the price once he locks in his supplies. Such a problem might in theory prevent the establishment of production of that commodity in a region, even if it would be profitable under competitive pricing. In that situation the potential monopsonist would actually welcome legal constraints on its exercise of market power.

When the source of local market power is a kind of natural local monopoly or oligopoly due to transport costs and economies of size, the usual antitrust protections are of little relevance, and encouraging entry is inefficient because it increases average cost. Because of a mismatch in the optimal size of the managerial unit, the alternative solution of vertical integration is also inefficient.

Other approaches to alleviating the problem include direct public control, as in state marketing boards such as the Canadian Wheat Board, or the formation of growers' cooperatives. In the United States antitrust exemptions and tax advantages encourage the latter. Although cooperatives and marketing boards have efficiency problems of their own, the case for some public encouragement of farmer cooperatives as protection against monopolization of farmers deserves consideration in formulating a new agricultural policy.

Collecting and Disseminating Information

Farmers, input suppliers, and processors need information on markets, regulations, and technology. Governments need information to execute their programs. Consumers benefit from being well informed about the price and quality of the goods they buy. Taxpayers and voters need information to know where their money should be and is being spent and what effect the spending is having.

In the language of economists, information is a public good. It is difficult to prevent people from using it without paying, and it is inefficient to make them pay more than the cost of making information available for one more user, which is usually very low or zero and less than the average cost per user. So there is an economic argument for the public provision of information when the number of potential users is large, as in agriculture.[4]

It is easy to understand why the government has traditionally provided farmers with large amounts of data about production, consumption, and marketing of their output, as well as about new technologies. But why is information on the effectiveness of government expen-

---

4. For the same reason, large corporations charge internal data services to overhead rather than bill internal users directly for the use of the data.

ditures in fulfilling the goals of farm policy so sparse? For example, as noted above, the government spends billions of dollars annually in the name of risk protection, but spends virtually nothing to verify the effects of that expenditure on the stability of the consumption of farm families.

A new agricultural program should include the public provision—perhaps using private contractors in some cases—of relevant information for producers and consumers. Dissemination of the information to farm households by computer will likely become so cheap that the use of a private on-line service for communication of that information will be quite efficient. Government should also collect information necessary for designing and executing its own policies.

I also propose a novel initiative: a requirement in the new farm bill that recipients of government support provide any data necessary for assessing the effects of that support. And no public program should be approved without the provision for the independent assessment—outside the Department of Agriculture—using modern economic theory, statistics, and econometrics as appropriate, of the program's effectiveness with respect to explicitly stated goals. Those assessments should themselves be available as public information.

Protecting Health, Safety, and Quality

The protection of health, safety, and quality covers animals, foods, feeds, workers, and consumers. Experience shows that industries have difficulties in policing themselves, hence the role for public assurance of performance. A related study in the AEI series on agricultural policy, *Choice and Efficiency in Food Safety Policy* by John M. Antle, addresses that issue.

8
Conclusion

Government plays an indispensable role in the U.S. agricultural sector. An important part of its contribution consists of providing general infrastructure, including roads, waterways, irrigation facilities, legal structures, and communications. But a large part is sector-specific. A farm bill written on a clean slate, unconstrained by previous policy, would likely contain measures recognizably similar to important parts of the current policy structure. Those include the support for agricultural research, the protection of farmers from anticompetitive exploitation, the protection of health and safety, the provision of relevant information, assistance for domestic food consumption by poor children and their mothers, food security measures including those for some grain stocks, and the encouragement of the holding of reserve production capacity.

A farm bill written anew should closely target conservation measures to emerging environmental requirements. In anticipation of the further evolution of environmental demands on farmers, some experiments with positive decentralized incentives rather than coercive regulation for certain activities such as species preservation would seem appropriate as a prelude to more extensive measures in later farm bills.

New farm policy legislation would depart radically from the current policy structure. The huge and expensive programs for price supports, market stabilization, and credit provision that dominate current farm policy would have no place. They have no adequate justification on commonly accepted grounds of efficiency and equity. Because of capitalization, income transfers by means of price supports or subsidies cannot significantly improve the attractiveness of farming in the long run, and they are also inequitable within and between generations of farmers. Because farmers' consumption has been observed to be quite effectively buffered against income fluctuations by savings, borrowing, and various types of diversification, public crop insurance and market stabilization policies are unnecessary, and indeed crop insurance is not popular in the absence of substantial subsidies. Farm credit is available on competitive terms from private sources; no public program would be needed in a new policy structure, beyond perhaps the services of Farmer Mac as a parallel to Ginnie Mae and Fannie Mae.

Although this policy structure would be new, the farm sector would look very familiar. Chemical inputs would be lower, the crop mix might be a little more diverse, productivity would be higher, and government expenditure would be substantially lower. Family farming would remain the overwhelmingly dominant managerial form, and policy would be on the road to adapting to evolving environmental demands.

What I have sketched here is by no means a sneak preview of the 1995 farm bill. The 1995 farm bill will have much more in common with the 1990 bill than with the structure outlined above. Why? Partly because the infeasibility, redundancy, or irrelevance of some of the most popular goals of agricultural policy are not widely perceived. And partly because the dead hand of past policies lies heavy on the process. Farmers would suffer a capital loss if past policies were brought in line with the kind of policy goals that farmers and the rest of the public might otherwise recognize as equitable and efficient.

That does not mean that piecemeal and gradual improvement is not possible, as the most recent negotiations on the General Agreement on Tariffs and Trade have demonstrated. And, given sufficient public comprehension of the issues, an unanticipated opportunity for wholesale reform just might arise, as the New Zealand experience shows.

References

Akerlof, George A., and Paul M. Romer. "Looting: The Economic Underworld of Bankruptcy for Profit." *Brookings Papers on Economic Activity* 2 (1993): 1–60.

Alderman, H., and Christina H. Paxson. "Do the Poor Insure? A Synthesis of the Literature on Risk-Bearing Institutions in Developing Countries." Memorandum. Washington, D.C.: World Bank, 1992.

Antle, John M. *Choice and Efficiency in Food Safety Policy.* Washington, D.C.: AEI Press, 1995.

Boehlje, Michael, Marvin Duncan, and David Lins. "Agricultural and Rural Finance Policy." In *The 1995 Farm Bill Policy Options and Consequences,* edited by Ronald D. Knutson. College Station: Texas Agricultural Extension Service, November 1994.

Browne, William P., Jerry R. Skees, Louis E. Swanson, Paul B. Thompson, and Laurian J. Unnevehr. *Sacred Cows and Hot Potatoes: Agrarian Myths in Agricultural Policy.* Boulder, Colo.: Westview Press, 1992.

Chamley, Christophe, and Brian D. Wright. "Fiscal Incidence in an Overlapping Generations Model with a Fixed Asset." *Journal of Public Economics* 32 (February 1987): 3–24.

Falk, Barry. "Formally Testing the Present Value Model of Farmland Prices." *American Journal of Agricultural Economics* 76 (February 1994): 1–10.

Fisher, Dennis U., Robert R. Fletcher, Thomas R. Harris, and Adell Brown, Jr. "Rural Development Policy." In *The 1995 Farm Bill Policy Options and Consequences,* edited by Ronald D. Knutson. College Station: Texas Agricultural Extension Service, November 1994.

Frengley, Gerald A. G., and Warren E. Johnston. "Financial Stress and Consumption Expectations among Farm Households: New Zealand's Experience with Economic Liberalization." *Journal of Agricultural Economics* 43 (January 1992): 14–27.

Goodwin, Barry K., and Vincent H. Smith. *The Economics of Crop Insurance and Disaster Aid.* Washington, D.C.: AEI Press, 1995.

Hazell, Peter, Carlos Pomareda, and Alberto Valdés, eds. *Crop Insurance for Agricultural Development.* Baltimore: Johns Hopkins University Press, 1986.

Huffman, Wallace E., and Robert E. Evenson. *Science for Agriculture: A Long-Term Perspective.* Ames: Iowa State University Press, 1993.

Iowa Farm Bill Study Team. "The Findings of the 1995 Farm Bill Study Team." Report, Iowa Farm Bureau, 1994.

Johnston, Warren E., and Gerald A. G. Frengley. "Economic Adjustments and Changes in Financial Viability of the Farming Sector: The New Zealand Experience." Paper presented at the American Agricultural Economics Association 1994 Annual Meeting, San Diego, Calif., August 9, 1994.

Just, Richard E., and Wallace E. Huffman. "Economic Principles and Incentives: Structure, Management, and Funding of Agricultural Research in the United States." *American Journal of Agricultural Economics* 74 (1992): 1101–8.

Kinsey, Jean, and Christine Ranney. "Food Assistance Policy." In *The 1995 Farm Bill Policy Options and Consequences,* edited by Ronald D. Knutson. College Station: Texas Agricultural Extension Service, November 1994.

Kislev, Yoav, and Willis Peterson. "Prices, Technology, and Farm Size." *Journal of Political Economy* 90 (1982): 578–95.

Langemeier, Michael R., and George F. Patrick. "Farmers' Marginal Propensity to Consume: An Application to Illinois Grain Farmers." *American Journal of Agricultural Economics* 72 (1990): 309–25.

Luloff, A. E., and Louis E. Swanson, eds. *American Rural Communities*. Boulder, Colo.: Westview Press, 1990.

McCloskey, Donald N. "English Open Fields as Behavior towards Risk." In *Research in Economic History*, vol. 1, edited by P. Uselding. Greenwich, Conn.: JAI Press, 1976.

Melichar, Emanuel. "Capital Gains versus Current Income in the Farming Sector." *American Journal of Agricultural Economics* 61 (December 1979): 1085–92.

Nerlove, Marc. "Reflections on the Economic Organization of Agriculture: Traditional, Modern, and Transitional." Report. College Park: University of Maryland, Department of Agricultural and Resource Economics, July 6, 1994.

Paxson, Christina H. "Using Weather Variability to Estimate the Response of Savings to Transitory Income in Thailand." *American Economic Review* 82 (1992): 15–33.

Ray, Daryll E. "The Economic Setting for U.S. Agriculture." In *The 1995 Farm Bill Policy Options and Consequences*, edited by Ronald D. Knutson. College Station: Texas Agricultural Extension Service, November 1994.

Sandrey, Ron, and Russell Reynolds, eds. *Farming without Subsidies: New Zealand's Recent Experience*. Wellington: New Zealand Ministry of Agriculture and Fisheries, 1990.

Swanson, Louis E. "Rethinking Assumptions about Farm and Community." In *American Rural Communities*, edited by A. E. Luloff and Louis E. Swanson. Boulder, Colo.: Westview Press, 1990.

U.S. Congress, Office of Technology Assessment. *Technology, Public Policy, and the Changing Structure of American Agriculture*. OTA-F-285. Washington, D.C.: Government Printing Office, March 1986.

U.S. General Accounting Office. "Conservation Reserve Program Cost-Effectiveness Is Uncertain." Report No. GAO/RCED-93-132. Washington, D.C.: Government Printing Office, March 1993.

Walker, Thomas S., and N. S. Jodha. "How Small Farm

Households Adapt to Risk." In *Crop Insurance for Agricultural Development Issues and Experience*, edited by Peter Hazell, Carlos Pomareda, and Alberto Valdés. Baltimore: Johns Hopkins University Press, 1986.

Webb, Alan J., Michael Lopez, and Renata Penn. *Estimates of Producer and Consumer Subsidy Equivalents: Government Intervention in Agriculture, 1982–87.* Statistical Bulletin No. 803. Washington, D.C.: U.S. Department of Agriculture, Economic Research Service, 1990.

Wright, Brian D. "Policy Regimes, Market Disturbances and Food Security." In *Improving Agricultural Trade Performance under the GATT*, edited by Tilman Becker, Richard Gray, and Andrew Schmitz. Kiel, Germany: Wissenschaftsverlag Vauk, 1992.

Wright, Brian D. "Public Insurance of Private Risks: Theory and Evidence from Agriculture." In *Government Risk-Bearing: Proceedings of a Conference Held at the Federal Reserve Bank of Cleveland, May 1991*, edited by Mark S. Sniderman. Boston: Kluwer Academic Publishers, 1993.

Wright, Brian D., and Julie A. Hewitt. "All-Risk Crop Insurance: Lessons from Theory and Experience." In *Economics of Agricultural Crop Insurance: Theory and Evidence*, edited by Darrell L. Heuth and William H. Furtan. Boston: Kluwer Academic Publishers, 1994.

Practical Policy Alternatives for the 1995 Farm Bill

Bruce L. Gardner

9
The 1995 Farm Bill

Innumerable possibilities exist for changes in U.S. farm programs in 1995. Detailed issues left unresolved in the Food, Agriculture, Conservation, and Trade Act of 1990 and changed economic conditions since 1990 invite many small adjustments. In aggregate those adjustments are important. But for purposes of this analysis they are mostly not individually important enough to justify the space needed to consider each one carefully. Other possibilities, such as replacing current programs with revenue insurance or subsidized put options, are too large. Each requires a major analytical effort, beyond the scope of this study.

This analysis considers a set of options that make a noticeable difference for the main commodities, yet are reachable from current policy and have visible political support. The main areas I address are market support prices, farm production flexibility and supply management, budgetary savings, and a broader group of industrial policy ideas. But before considering the pros and cons of policy options in those areas, I shall review economic successes achieved and failures endured along the policy path to this point. Then we shall be in a better position to choose where to go next.

I would like to acknowledge the valuable detailed comments on earlier drafts received from Julian Alston, John Campbell, Stanley Johnson, Andrew Morton, and Daniel A. Sumner.

10
Economic Situation and Baseline for Policy Options

Twenty years ago U.S. agriculture was in the midst of the century's greatest peacetime commodity price boom. Price support programs became largely redundant. The Sugar Act was allowed to lapse, and payments to grain and cotton producers largely ceased. Governmental regulation was most notable in attempting to keep some farm prices from rising, through export controls on soybeans and grains. After decades of attempts to hold farm production down, farmers were urged to "plant fencerow to fencerow." Increases in farmland prices indicated a belief that a new era of agricultural prosperity had dawned.

But by the late 1970s it became plausible, and by the early 1980s practically certain, that underlying conditions had not significantly changed. Commodity prices retreated to their long-term trend of roughly a 1.5 percent annual decline in real terms, reflecting productivity growth primarily (figure 10–1). Unfortunately, the transition from the euphoric 1970s was not a smooth one for farmers. Those who borrowed at high interest rates to buy land in the late 1970s and early 1980s were particularly vulnerable. They constituted the core of the farm crisis that made agriculture's problems national news and the subject of several major movies in the mid-1980s. It was only at the end of the 1980s that farm income and land prices returned to their apparently more stable longer-term trend (figure 10–2).

FIGURE 10–1
REAL FARM PRICES, 1950–1993
(index: 1987 = 100)

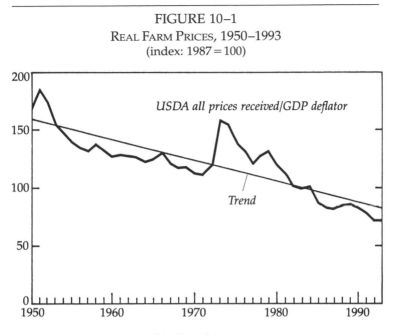

SOURCE: *Economic Report of the President.*

As farm incomes declined in the late 1970s, the federal government moved quickly to reinvent farm policy. The Ford administration increased Commodity Credit Corporation loan rates, which support market prices, during the 1976 presidential campaign. The Carter administration recommended substantial increases in target prices, which determine the level of deficiency payments to producers, and Congress exceeded the recommended increases in the four-year Food and Agriculture Act of 1977. In response to the most strident show of farmer discontent in the post–World War II era, Congress in 1978 amended that legislation with further acreage controls, commodity storage programs, emergency Farmers Home Administration loans, and other measures to boost farm income. In the Agriculture and Food Act of 1981, the Reagan administration, backed by a Re-

73

FIGURE 10–2
FARM INCOME AND LAND PRICE, 1971–1993
(1987 dollars)

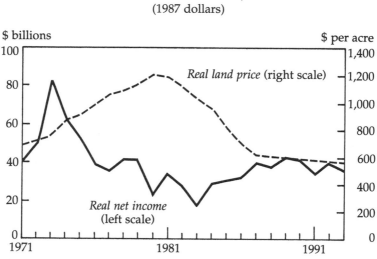

SOURCE: *Economic Report of the President.*

publican Senate and an antigovernment ideology, managed only to increase target prices and loan rates further. In 1977 the Commodity Credit Corporation removed 6.9 billion pounds of surplus milk from the market at a support price of $9.00 per hundredweight. By the end of 1982, the support price had risen to $13.10, at which price fourteen billion pounds of surplus milk were purchased in 1982 and seventeen billion pounds in 1983.

The data in table 10–1 summarize the general picture for the past twenty-five years on budget outlays for farm price and income support. Following low outlays in fiscal years 1974 through 1976, the level of spending to support agriculture rose to record highs (both nominal and real) from 1982 through 1988 and currently remains above the levels from 1950 through 1970. Indeed, the level of spending in the peak years of the New Deal farm programs was less than $2 billion (in 1987 dollars), compared with $13 billion to $14 billion in 1993 and 1994. From 1991 through 1994, with a more nearly normalized

TABLE 10-1
AGRICULTURAL BUDGET OUTLAYS AND IDLED CROPLAND, 1970-1994

Fiscal Year[a]	Agricultural Budget Outlays[b] ($ billions)	Real Agricultural Outlays ($ billions)[c]	Idled Acres (millions)
1970	4.6	13.0	57
1971	3.7	9.8	37
1972	4.6	11.7	62
1973	4.1	9.9	19
1974	1.5	3.2	3
1975	2.2	4.4	2
1976	2.2	4.3	2
1977	5.7	10.3	0
1978	10.2	17.0	16
1979	9.9	15.1	11
1980	7.4	10.4	0
1981	9.8	12.4	0
1982	14.3	17.1	12
1983	21.3	24.5	77
1984	11.9	13.1	27
1985	23.8	25.2	31
1986	29.6	30.6	48
1987	24.7	24.7	76
1988	15.2	14.7	62
1989	14.8	13.7	58
1990	9.8	8.6	58
1991	12.9	11.0	49
1992	12.5	10.3	50*
1993	18.9	15.2	52*
1994	15.0	11.8	44*

*Author's estimates. Includes thirty-six million acres in the Conservation Reserve Program.
a. Fiscal year 1994 runs from October 1, 1993, to September 30, 1994.
b. Subfunction 351, Farm Income Stabilization, in the Budget of the United States.
c. Deflated by the implicit GDP deflator, 1987 = 100.
SOURCES: Budget of the United States; U.S. Department of Agriculture.

economic situation under the current farm legislation, we find ourselves spending on agriculture at about the 1970 through 1972 level in real terms. Indeed, real spending is higher currently if we include the Conservation Reserve Program, which is omitted from farm program spending in the Office of Management and Budget's accounting. That program, which did not exist in the 1970s, cost about $1.8 billion annually in 1993 and 1994.

A second indicator of government action to support farm income, but at the expense of food consumers rather than taxpayers, is the number of cropland acres held idle under farm programs. That indicator also climbed to record heights in the mid-1980s and has now returned roughly to 1970 through 1972 levels.

The farm population is now about half what it was in 1970. So support to agriculture per capita is historically even higher now—only topped by the extraordinary spending efforts of 1983 through 1987. Some have wondered whether taxpayers will continue their willingness to pay up at those rates. On the other hand, the agriculture committees of Congress have reminded their colleagues that agriculture has taken a substantial budget cut in the Clinton and Bush budget reduction efforts, especially in 1990, when the Omnibus Budget Reconciliation Act introduced "mandatory flex" acreage—15 percent of each farmer's payment acreage on which the farmer could plant any program crop, or a few nonprogram crops, but on which no payments would be made. That and other provisions were scored as a $13 billion budget cut for agriculture over five years.

Those reductions have not materialized, and it is worth reviewing the reasons in detail. Congressional debate on proposed programs in agriculture typically is conducted with reference to a baseline. Each option's effects on budget outlays, commodity prices, farm income, and other variables are compared with budget outlays under a current policy baseline. Thus, currently legislated target prices, loan rates, and related policy instruments are continued. Specifying that baseline is not so

FIGURE 10–3

COMMODITY CREDIT CORPORATION ACTUAL AND PROJECTED NET
OUTLAYS, 1988–1995

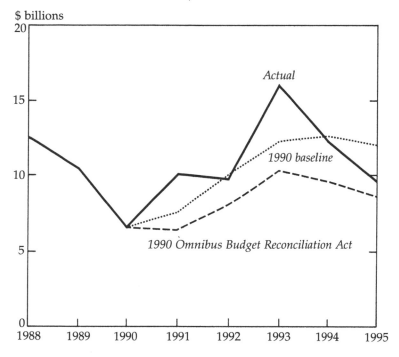

SOURCE: U.S. Department of Agriculture, *Agricultural Outlook.*

simple as might at first be thought, because program parameters, such as percentages of acreage required to be
idled by program participants, vary annually according
to market conditions. The Congressional Budget Office,
OMB, and private institutions such as the Food and Agricultural Policy Research Institute construct detailed
year-by-year, commodity-by-commodity baselines—in
the case of a five-year farm bill, for five years into the
future.

Figure 10–3 shows how savings were measured in
1990. The fiscal year 1990 level of Commodity Credit
Corporation outlays (most but not all of the spending

shown in table 10–1) was $6.5 billion. The 1990 Omnibus Budget Reconciliation Act was not intended to reduce spending from that level. Instead, savings were scored from the existing baseline spending level shown as "1990 baseline" in figure 10–3. The policy changes introduced generated the projected spending shown as "1990 Omnibus Budget Reconciliation Act." Cumulating the vertical distances between the 1990 baseline and 1990 Omnibus Budget Reconciliation Act projections over fiscal years 1991 through 1995 yields the $13 billion savings claimed (as part of the $500 billion deficit reduction claimed for the Bush budget agreement of 1990).

Actual spending and late-1994 projections are shown as "actual" in figure 10–3. Not only did the Omnibus Budget Reconciliation Act savings not make it to the bank, but we have ended up spending more than the pre-Omnibus Budget Reconciliation Act baseline! The projections and data used in figure 10–3 are those of the U.S. Department of Agriculture and the OMB, as reported in *Agricultural Outlook* (USDA 1994c, 56). Also, CBO scoring differs in a few ways. Table 10–2 presents CBO data on 1990 Omnibus Budget Reconciliation Act savings and also an accounting for effects of some policy changes since 1990. Actual Commodity Credit Corporation outlays exceed the post-1990 Omnibus Budget Reconciliation Act baseline by $16 billion from 1991 through 1995. This is an even worse performance than the USDA-OMB data indicate.

Table 10–2 also includes two items to help explain why outlays exceeded the baseline. First, policy changes caused part of the increase. From 1991 through 1995, Congress made $5.8 billion in appropriations for crop disaster assistance that were not in the baseline. Those more than offset additional savings made in the 1993 Omnibus Budget Reconciliation Act and other appropriations reductions in 1993 and 1994. Second, an accounting change was made. Starting in fiscal year 1992, administrative expenses such as payroll and equipment of the Agricultural Stabilization and Conservation Ser-

TABLE 10–2
CONGRESSIONAL BUDGET OFFICE PROJECTIONS OF COMMODITY
CREDIT CORPORATION SPENDING, 1991–1995
($ billions)

	Fiscal Year					
	1991	1992	1993	1994	1995	1991–95
(1) Pre-1990 Omnibus Budget Reconciliation Act (FY91 budget resolution baseline)	8.6	11.5	11.0	10.5	9.9	52
(2) 1990 OBRA and farm act	−1.5	−3.2	−2.3	−2.3	−2.5	−12
(3) Post-OBRA baseline: (1) − (2)	7.1	8.3	8.7	8.2	7.4	40
(4) Actual Commodity Credit Corporation outlays	10.1	9.7	16.0	10.3	10.5[a]	57
(5) Excess of actual over projected: (4) − (3)	3.0	1.4	7.3	2.1	3.1	17
Factors accounting for excess of actual over projected outlays:						
(6) Post-1990 legislation[b]	0	.9	.8	2.8	0	4
(7) Accounting change[c]	0	−.8	−.8	−.8	−.8	−3
(8) Remaining unexplained excess of spending over 1990 baseline: (5) − (6) − (7)	3.1	1.3	7.3	.1	3.9	16

a. Author's estimate.
b. Crop disaster appropriations, 1993 OBRA, wool program and export program reduction in 1993 and 1994.
c. Administrative expenses of the Agricultural Stabilization and Conservation Service shifted out of the CCC account.
SOURCE: Data from Senate Agriculture Committee, Republican staff.

vice were shifted out of the Commodity Credit Corporation's budget. Those expenses amount to $780 million per year (about $2,500 per U.S. commercial farmer). That, of course, is not a "saving" at all, and it means that the gap between expected and actual outlays from 1991 through 1995 is really about $3 billion higher than the earlier calculations indicate.

That experience and other Commodity Credit Corpo-

TABLE 10–3
COMMODITY CREDIT CORPORATION FISCAL YEAR NET
OUTLAYS BY COMMODITY
($ millions)

Commodity	1978	1986	1992	1993	1994
Wheat	844	3,440	1,719	2,185	1,972
Rice	−66	947	715	887	756
Cotton	224	2,142	1,443	2,239	1,496
Corn		10,524	2,105	5,143	635
Sorghum	2,288	1,185	190	410	133
Barley		471	174	186	237
Oats		26	32	16	6
Milk	240	2,337	232	253	237
Tobacco	98	253	29	235	641
Soybeans	31	1,597	−29	109	−162
Peanuts	−39	32	41	−13	38
Sugar	395	214	−14	−35	−25
Honey	3	89	17	22	10
Wool	33	123	191	179	210
Other[a]	1,608	2,461	2,900	4,231	5,608
Total	5,656	25,841	9,738	16,047	11,792

a. Operating and interest expenses, export programs, disaster programs, and Commodity Credit Corporation purchases of other commodities (but operating expenses are omitted after 1992).
SOURCE: U.S. Department of Agriculture.

ration outlay underestimates of the 1980s show that the budgetary assessment of policy options has serious pitfalls. To obtain a sense of what they are, and to establish more detailed background for considering policy options, let us turn to the situation of particular commodities.

Table 10–3 shows Commodity Credit Corporation outlays for several commodities in selected recent years. Corn and wheat account for 40 to 50 percent of all farm program outlays. Milk and cotton have cost over $1 billion in some years. Other commodities are less important in the aggregate but still indicate very substantial intervention in the smaller markets. Wool payments averaged

$185 million in 1992 and 1993, three times the market value of the wool. Rice payments per unit of output have been higher per unit of output than was the case for wheat or corn over the past decade.

Moreover, some commodities have programs that assist producers much more than the Commodity Credit Corporation outlays indicate. Tobacco has had a series of "no net cost" laws and regulations under which the government's price support costs are to be offset by assessments against tobacco producers and buyers. But production controls still maintain the tobacco price well above free-market levels. Sugar likewise has low Commodity Credit Corporation costs, but only because import restrictions keep the domestic price of sugar above the Commodity Credit Corporation's support level, which is about double the world price. Consequently, consumers pay $3 billion to $5 billion annually in addition to the taxpayer costs of supporting farm commodities (Gardner 1991; Lin 1989).

Corn

To see more specifically the linkages between commodity program parameters and government outlays, consider the recent history and current projections for corn. The target price for corn, after rising about 30 percent between 1978 and 1984, was cut in the Food Security Act of 1985 from $3.03 to $2.75 per bushel, starting in 1988 (see figure 10–4). The 1990 legislation introduced a provision by which 15 percent of each farmer's acreage base would receive no payments. About 5 billion bushels of corn were eligible for payments from 1992 through 1994, even though production at normal yields is about 8.5 billion bushels. There are three reasons for that difference. First, payments are made only on "program yield," which is fixed at levels determined in the early 1980s, about 104 bushels per acre, compared with the average U.S. yield of about 120 bushels per acre (Westcott 1993). Second, some farmers do not participate in the corn program;

FIGURE 10–4

CORN PRICES AND PAYMENTS, 1978–1996

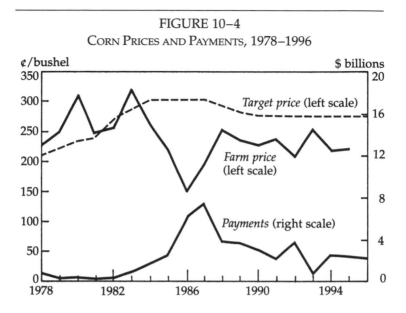

SOURCE: U.S. Department of Agriculture.

nonparticipants operate about 20 percent of the U.S. corn payment acreage base. Third, there is a 15 percent non-payment acreage plus a requirement that participants leave zero to 10 percent of their corn base idle under the acreage reduction program and receive no payments for corn that could have been produced on the acreage. Even if the farmer cheated and grew corn on acreage reduction program land, no payments would be made on that acreage.

Deficiency payments have been made on the difference between the target price and the average U.S. farm-level market price from September through January of each year. If a farm sells corn for more or less than the average market price, the payment the farm receives is unchanged.[1] Therefore, since the five-month price has

---

1. If farmers switch to selling outside the five-month period, they still receive payments based on the five-month price. That is impor-

been below the target price in each of the past ten years, *all* corn program participants have received payments.

With a six billion bushel payment base, cutting the target price from $3.03 to $2.75 reduces annual government outlays by $1.68 billion. Thus, the 1985 act changes were not trivial. The 1990 reductions are more difficult to quantify because they depend on the market price. In 1990 analysts expected market prices for the early 1990s to average about $2.15 per bushel—indicating payments of $3.6 billion. A 15 percent reduction of the 6 billion bushels, to 5.1 billion bushels, would therefore save $540 million in annual outlays. In addition, the 1990 act changed the market price used in calculating deficiency payments from a five-month to a twelve-month basis in such a way that deficiency payments would be reduced by seven cents per bushel (and not more or less) from the five-month approach in effect through 1992. That change saved an additional $36 million annually. Therefore, the sum of corn policy changes since 1985 reduced deficiency payments by about $2.6 billion annually.

So why did corn deficiency payments in fiscal year 1993 go up to $5.1 billion—accounting for much of the excess over the baseline shown in figure 10–3 for that year? The most important reason is that the five-month price of corn from the 1992 crop (September 1992 through January 1993) was $2.02, about twenty cents per bushel below the baseline level. That added about $1 billion in outlays. A similar result is likely in fiscal year 1995. The main causes are the record large corn production in 1992 and again in 1994. On the other hand, the five-month price for the 1993 crop was above the baseline

---

tant because prices typically rise later in the marketing year. In the 1990 crop year the estimated price for all corn sold was $2.28, while the five-month price was $2.24 (giving a deficiency payment rate of $.51). So it could be argued that for the average farmer the effective target price was $2.79 instead of $2.75, since receipts for an average bushel were $2.79.

level owing to the short crop caused by extraordinarily wet weather in the Midwest, so outlays will be below the baseline in fiscal year 1994.[2]

Generally, the 1990 corn baseline has held up fairly well, and mid-1994 baseline price forecasts (by both the Food and Agricultural Policy Research Institute and the USDA) for 1995 through 1998 remain in the $2.20 to $2.25 neighborhood. Futures prices for 1995 delivery also indicate (as of late 1994) that same range of expected prices for the 1994 and 1995 crops (slightly lower for 1994 and slightly higher for 1995). The analysis of policy options below uses those baseline prices as a reference point for comparing alternative policy options.

The 1990 baseline was not, however, quite so accurate as the price projections indicate. The reason is that the acreage reduction program provisions mentioned earlier make price forecasting easier. If a low-price scenario unfolds, with rising carryover stocks, then the 1990 act requires the secretary of agriculture to increase acreage reduction programs. If, however, increased demand or short supplies emerge, acreage reduction programs can be decreased. The 1989 through 1990 baseline had corn acreage reduction programs of 7.5 to 10 percent in the mid-1990s. Actually, the corn acreage reduction program was cut to 5 percent in 1992 and to zero in 1994. That reflects increases in demand for corn (weaker export demand by about 30 percent but more than offsetting strength in domestic demand) compared with

---

2. The corn outlay figures in table 10–2 differ from those plotted in figure 10–4 because the table shows fiscal year data while the figure shows outlays spent for a particular year's crop. Thus, fiscal year 1993 shows advance payments (mandated by Congress) on the 1994 crop as well as payments on the 1993 crop above the advance payments on that crop that were made in fiscal year 1992. Both the crop-specific and fiscal-year figures are official USDA data. It would be simpler to use only fiscal-year or crop-specific data, but they would fail to expose the reader to some of the relevant complexity of current farm programs and budget scoring.

FIGURE 10–5
WHEAT PRICES AND PAYMENTS, 1978–1995

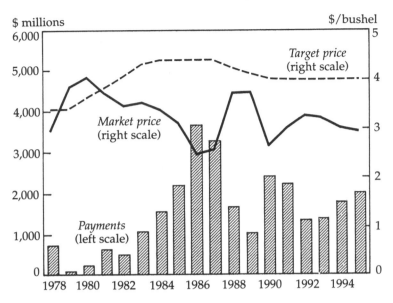

SOURCE: U.S. Department of Agriculture.

earlier anticipation and the short crop of 1993. The Food and Agricultural Policy Research Institute 1994 baseline projects a 7.5 percent corn acreage reduction program for each year from 1995 through 1998.

Wheat

The story of wheat policy is similar to that of corn, with a little higher level of policy intensity (figure 10–5). While wheat payments have been lower than corn payments, the volume of wheat production is only about one-third that of corn. Wheat receives substantially more per dollar of market value, basically because the wheat target price exceeds the recent wheat market price by about 30 percent, while the corn target price exceeds the corn market price by about 20 percent.

In addition, wheat has received favored treatment

85

through a delayed introduction of the nonpayment base and from about $1 billion annually in export subsidies under the export enhancement program. Wheat is concentrated in the highly rural states of the Great Plains, and the representatives and senators of those areas appear to devote more of their energy to wheat (for example, by being active on the agriculture committees) than the Corn Belt representatives do for corn. Plus, Senator Robert Dole of Kansas, as the Senate's minority leader until 1995, was able to ensure that wheat was not neglected, even if the Committee on Agriculture, Nutrition, and Forestry did not fully accomplish that goal. Nonetheless, the grains—barley and sorghum grain, as well as wheat and corn—have all had the same basic experience: a 9 percent target price cut in the 1985 act and a 15 percent payment acreage cut in 1990.

Wheat is also more heavily affected than corn by the Conservation Reserve Program, a scheme to hold cropland in grasses or other conservation uses under ten-year contracts with farmers. Initiated in the 1985 act, that program now has 36.5 million acres enrolled, of which farmers have designated eleven million acres for wheat. If we assume that the land enrolled would generate 90 percent of the yield of land idled annually under acreage reduction programs, the Conservation Reserve Program is roughly equivalent to a 15 percent acreage reduction program. Thus, although the acreage reduction program percentage in 1994 is zero, wheat acreage is being held out of production as if the acreage reduction program were 15 percent. It should be noted that, unlike acreage reduction programs, the Conservation Reserve Program pays farmers a cash rental for participation that averages about $50 per acre. Those rentals are not included in Commodity Credit Corporation wheat payments shown in table 10–2 and figure 10–5. Thus, wheat producers now receive about $500 million annually above the amounts shown there.

In addition, a substantial amount of wheat land—4.7 million acres in 1994—is enrolled in the 0–92 program, in which payments are made on idled acres beyond the 15 percent nonpayment base. Some of that acreage is planted to minor oilseeds (sunflower, safflower, canola, rapeseed, flaxseed, or mustard seed) or to certain experimental crops, which legislation permits to be planted on wheat land while farmers continue to receive wheat payments. Such oilseeds are ineligible, however, for the minor oilseed price support that Congress introduced in the 1990 act.

Cotton

Cotton has the same target price structure as the grains and has taken the same cuts in 1985 and 1992 (figure 10–6). Cotton, however, has enjoyed additional benefits that make producers' protection even more substantial than for corn or wheat. The target price exceeds the 1992 average farm price by 35 percent. Moreover, cotton also receives loan deficiency payments.

The extra payments are made under a marketing loan program. The cotton program, like the wheat program, holds the U.S. price above the price at which the product can be profitably exported to most of the world. Wheat is made competitive by means of export subsidies. Cotton is made competitive by granting loan deficiency payments to producers who forgo Commodity Credit Corporation loans. The payment, made to both domestically used and exported cotton, is equal to the difference between the loan support price (52.35 cents per pound in 1993 for a reference grade of cotton at the average U.S. location) and a loan repayment rate, which is determined weekly. The loan repayment rate is the higher of the adjusted world price for the week or 70 percent of the loan rate. The USDA determines the adjusted world price weekly on the basis of market prices in Northern Europe.

87

FIGURE 10-6
COTTON PRICES AND PAYMENTS, 1978–1995

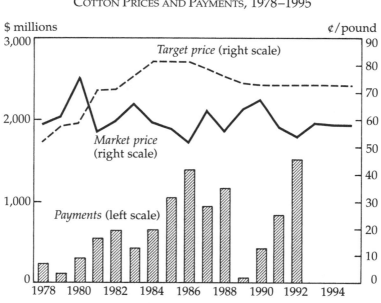

SOURCE: U.S. Department of Agriculture.

The government makes an additional payment in the form of marketing certificates when price quotes for types of cotton in the United States exceed the North European price. Those payments go to domestic users and exporters, but because they increase the value of U.S. cotton, they amount to a producer subsidy in a competitive market setting. In 1992 deficiency payments were $1,019 million, loan deficiency payments were $275 million, and user certificates were $210 million. The total of $1.5 billion amounts to 19.5 cents per pound of cotton produced or 35 percent of the farm price. The payments over and above deficiency payments have raised an equity issue among grain producers who do not have that supplemental support (although rice does have an active marketing loan program).

Unlike the grains, the annual acreage reduction program for cotton was not reduced in 1993 and 1994. The

1994 cotton acreage reduction program remains at 11 percent. But very little cotton land is in the Conservation Reserve Program or is idled under the 0–92 program, and the total rate of acreage idling is slightly less for cotton than for wheat, despite wheat's zero acreage reduction program.

For all the feed grains, wheat, rice, and cotton, it is worth noting the escalation in already overly complex laws and regulatory provisions that occurred in the 1990 farm act, the 1990 Omnibus Budget Reconciliation Act, and the 1993 Omnibus Budget Reconciliation Act. The complexities were induced by the combination of desire for increased flexibility for farmers, budgetary savings, and environmental sensitivity—all to be done at the least possible cost to farm income and with special attention to formerly neglected crops such as minor oilseeds and raw materials for new uses of farm commodities. The USDA, for example, describes the determination of the deficiency payment for the 1994 wheat crop as follows:

> If the national weighted-average market price received by producers during the first *five* months of the marketing year (June 1994 through October 1994) plus 10 cents is below the *target price*, eligible producers will receive deficiency payments in December 1994, less any advance, equal to the difference between the target level and the higher of the five-month price plus 10 cents and the *basic* (statutory) loan rate—$2.72 per bushel. If the national weighted-average price received by producers during the first *twelve* months of the marketing year (June 1994 through May 1995) is less than the five-month price plus 10 cents, an additional payment will be made in July 1995, equal to the difference between the five-month price plus 10 cents and the higher of the 12-month price and the *basic* loan rate.
>
> Additional "Findley" payments, if they are earned, will be paid to eligible producers in July

1995, less any advances, equal to the difference between the basic loan rate and the higher of the 12-month price and the *announced* national average loan rate ($2.58).

Producers may elect, at sign-up time, to receive a minimum of 75 percent of any projected additional "Findley" deficiency payment on December 1, 1994, based on a December 1, 1994, estimate of the season average market price.

Payments will be determined by multiplying the payment rate times the farm payment acreage times the farm program payment yield.

The 1994 farm program payment yield remains at the 1993 level. However, if a farm has had both irrigated and nonirrigated payment yields for a crop, the 1994 payment yield will reflect the history of irrigating and not whether the payment acreage is actually irrigated in 1994.

If the payment yield for a crop is less than 90 percent of the equivalent yield in 1985, producers will be compensated to ensure they receive the same return as if the yield had not been reduced by more than 10 percent.

For the 1994 crop and subsequent years, irrigated yields will not be established on any acreage not having an irrigated yield prior to the 1986 crop year.

Deficiency payment acreage is the lower of the acreage actually planted to wheat or the maximum payment acreage [85 percent of the farm's wheat base]. However, producers may underplant their maximum payment acreage and still, under some conditions, receive deficiency payments. Wheat producers may devote all or a portion of the maximum payment acreage to Conserving Uses (CU), and receive minimum guaranteed deficiency payments on the acres designated in excess of required non-payment acres. The payment rate will be the higher of the projected or actual deficiency rate for the wheat program crop.

Required non-payment acres normally are 15 percent of maximum payment acreage. Exceptions for wheat which allow producers to reduce their required non-payment acres below 15 percent of maximum payment acreage are provided to producers who designate acreage exceeding 8 percent of the maximum payment acreage to minor oilseeds, industrial and other crops, or when the acreage of the crop was prevented from being planted or failed and was subsequently devoted to conserving uses for payment.

Note that "minor" oilseeds such as sunflower seed, safflower, canola, rapeseed, flaxseed or mustard seed, may be planted on the [wheat] land and qualify for payments. However, if payments are received, the oilseed crop becomes ineligible for price support loan for all of that oilseed produced on the farm.

Soybeans may be planted on wheat acres following a minor oilseed crop. The producer must have a history of double-cropping soybeans following any other crop on the farm in three of the previous five years. Other restrictions may apply.

Dry peas and lentils may be planted on up to 20 percent of the wheat acreage base and receive planted and considered planted credit. No deficiency payments will be paid on acreage devoted to these crops.

The wheat acreage base is the average of planted and considered planted for the five-year period (1989–1993).

Producers who choose not to participate in any annual program and certify that no acreage on the farm was planted to the crop have two options for protecting their planted history: (1) the "zero certification" option allows them to have their entire program crop acreage base considered as planted for base retention purposes. However, they must certify that any fruits or vegetables planted on the farm were not in excess of normal plantings.

Haying and grazing will be permitted on the [set-aside] acreage and on the conserving uses for payment (including the 15 percent of qualifying acres), except during a consecutive five-month period between April 1 through October 31 (USDA 1994b, 4–5).

In addition, by January 1, 1995, all producers of program crops must have fully applied an approved conservation plan if they plant any agricultural crop on highly erodible land. Producers who do not have a USDA-approved plan or have not fully applied it by the deadline remain ineligible for USDA commodity programs until the USDA's Soil Conservation Service certifies that an approved plan is fully applied. Also, any person who plants a crop on a wetland converted to cropland after December 23, 1985, or who converted a wetland after November 28, 1990, is ineligible for USDA benefits. And, of course, program participants must comply with acreage reduction program requirements and stay within payment limits.

Many of those provisions have caused confusion and consternation and have created many difficulties in implementation, appeals, and resolution of disputed cases. Neither Congress nor the political decision makers in the executive branch have a clear idea of what they have done. The regulations for each crop are fully understood only by a few USDA specialists, congressional committee staff, and industry experts. It is doubtful that anyone in the universe has a complete grip on all the regulations for every commodity.

Milk

Milk is supported under another complicated system, quite different from the grains and cotton. Milk has no target price and, normally, no direct payments to farmers. Instead, the Commodity Credit Corporation supports the price of milk used to manufacture butter, nonfat dry milk, and cheese by purchasing those commodities. Congress sets the support price in terms of whole milk at the farm level. The USDA attempts to establish that as a price floor by means of standing offers to buy butter, nonfat dry milk, and cheese at prices that will result in milk plants' paying the support price to farmers. As of mid-1993, for example, the USDA paid sixty-five cents per pound of butter and $1.034 per pound of nonfat dry milk. Those would make the value of butter and powder in a hundred pounds of 3.67 percent butterfat milk $11.32. Allowing $1.22 per hundred pounds as the cost of making milk into butter (from the fat) and powder (from the nonfat solids) would generate a whole milk price of $10.10, as Congress mandated.

In the 1970s the support price of milk rose quite sharply (figure 10–7). By the early 1980s the Commodity Credit Corporation's removals—purchases minus sales later in the same year—amounted to about 10 percent of all U.S production. The Commodity Credit Corporation's stocks of cheese, butter, and nonfat milk were so large that in the 1980s Congress enacted various programs to distribute them as food assistance as well as two programs to reduce production. One comprised contracts with farmers in which they were paid to reduce output; the second was a buyout of whole herds.

Beginning in 1985, the support price was cut, and

FIGURE 10–7

Milk Prices and Commodity Credit Corporation Removals,
1975–1995

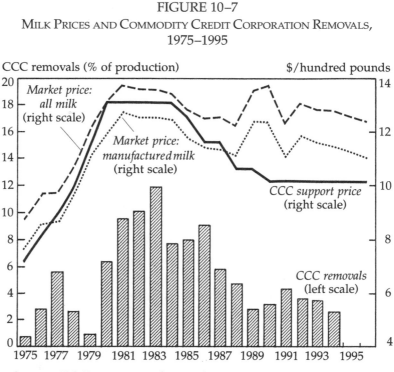

Source: U.S. Department of Agriculture.

by 1990 it had been reduced by 23 percent to $10.10 per hundred pounds, the level that still prevails. Under current law the support price will be increased at least twenty-five cents per hundredweight each year in which the USDA estimates purchases of less than 3.5 billion pounds. For 1994 those purchases were estimated at about four billion pounds.

The market price of manufacturing milk from 1991 through 1994 has been above the support price by about 15 percent, but even so the USDA has continued making purchases. That is the result of seasonal purchases in months—usually in the spring—when prices are low. Products that are later donated to domestic and foreign food assistance programs remain counted as net USDA removals. In addition, dairy products exported under the dairy export incentive program are counted as USDA purchases, although those exports are shipped directly from commercial sources without ever being in the hands of the USDA. In fiscal year 1993 domestic donations amounted to $226 million, foreign donations to $149 million, and dairy export incentive program export subsidies to $135 million, for a total cost of $510 million. The USDA's projected costs for calendar year 1995 are $557 million.

Dairy did not receive a cut in support in 1990 equivalent to the 15 percent reduction in payment acreage for grains and cotton. An assessment was, however, imposed on all producers who market more milk in any year, starting in 1991, than they did in the preceding year. In 1993 and 1994 that assessment averaged 1.1 percent of the support price (about 1.5 percent for producers who increased output and zero for those who reduced output and claimed a refund). The 1990 act also limits Commodity Credit Corporation expenditures to purchases of dairy products that are equivalent to seven billion pounds of milk, on a total (fat and nonfat) solids basis. If the USDA projects that Commodity Credit Corporation purchases will be greater than seven billion pounds (about 5 percent of production), an assessment on milk producers must be collected to cover the costs of purchases. In November 1994 the USDA estimated 1995 dairy purchases (including dairy export incentive program) at 6.4 billion pounds, so no 1995 assessment will be imposed.

As figure 10–7 shows, the average market price for all milk sold by farmers is higher, by about 12 percent, than the price of manufacturing milk. That occurs because about 40 percent of U.S. milk is sold for use in fluid milk products, at a price averaging about 25 percent above the manufacturing milk price. That price differential for physically identical classes of milk occurs because of the marketing order system, a separate component of dairy policy. Complicated regulations, enforced by the USDA, enable that price discrimination to persist. It is difficult to estimate how much effect that system has on the price of milk. Fluid milk even under competition would have a higher average price than manufacturing milk because more of it is produced in high-cost areas (notably the Southeast), to which it is costly to ship fluid milk from low-cost areas. Several independent estimates suggest that the marketing order system increases the average farm price of milk by about 4 percent (Dairy Policy Task Force 1986). The constancy of the differential between the two market prices plotted in figure 10–7 indicates that the price effect has been stable over the past twenty years.

11
Policy Options for 1995

The farm legislation of 1990, including outlay-reducing measures in the budget reconciliation act of that year, was the result of a lengthy and detailed political debate among many interested parties. The political decisions reached in 1995 will differ from the 1990 results only because of economic or political changes. Alternatives to current policies may be viable for four main reasons: changes in the political weight of various interest groups; changes in the economic situation of agriculture and in the general economy; lessons learned from implementing the 1990 act and subsequent legislation, as well as new information about the effects of continuing policies; and the development of new policy ideas.

Two key political facts are that voters elected a Democratic administration in 1992 and a Republican Congress in 1994. Under the Clinton administration, the USDA has become more heavily weighted with proponents of keeping market prices up. The secretary of agriculture has less vigorously used his discretion to keep Commodity Credit Corporation loan rates low, and loan support prices have increased.

Underlying the 1994 Republican victory is the fact that public mistrust of government and the desire for less taxation and spending remain strong and probably have increased. Those factors suggest further intense scrutiny of the farm income support budget.

Note also that the Clinton administration entered office to a persistent beat of environmental tom-toms. This, together with the fact that existing Conservation Reserve Program contracts will almost all expire between 1996 and 1999, has created a potential for change in the conservation-environmental aspects of commodity programs. It also gives oxygen to an agenda for subsidized technology, in sustainable agriculture, and a general increase in regulations (as in ethanol-use mandates) and public investment that can be summarized under the heading of industrial policy for agriculture. The 1994 election results are widely seen as damaging to environmental interests, but the effect on the broader industrial policy agenda, notably promotion of new uses for farm products, is less clear.

Another political fact is that the North American Free Trade Agreement, the most recent negotiations on the General Agreement on Tariffs and Trade, and continuing disputes between the countries involved have required changes in U.S. international policy. Some U.S. policy decisions may look different under the light of those agreements, and trade policies in particular will have to change.

Perhaps the foggiest political fact—concrete facts are not yet in place—is that rural representation in Congress, particularly in the House of Representatives, has continued to evolve and perhaps to weaken. The *New York Times* opened its season of reporting on the 1995 farm bill with a boost for hopes of radical change. The paper reported that "in recent years Federal money for subsidies has dropped precipitously, a measure of the long, slow erosion of farmers' political clout in Washington" (July 25, 1994, p. 1). But the reporter had not looked at the data shown in table 10–1, which indicate that agriculture has as much support now as it did twenty-five years ago and more on a per farm basis. The long, slow erosion continues to be of taxpayers' dollars, with farmers' catching the silt. Still, maybe 1995 will be different.

The economic situation has no compelling sources

of policy changes. The most notable development in 1994 was the end of a period of exceptionally profitable live-stock prices, especially for hogs. But there are no price support programs for meats, except relatively minor and sporadic export subsidies and import restrictions. Despite a record-large corn crop in 1994, the major program crops are not far from the economic conditions that were expected when Congress debated the 1990 act. Indeed, events have transpired much as projected in the USDA and Food and Agricultural Policy Research Institute baselines used at that time. The biggest departure from 1990 expectations has been in dairy. Milk prices were expected in 1990 to remain near the $10.10 support level over the 1991 to 1995 period and to require substantial Commodity Credit Corporation purchases to maintain that level. Congress was inclined to impose supply controls to support milk prices, but industry disagreements and Bush administration opposition apparently tipped the balance to only a study of supply control measures in 1990 that would lead to possible new policy in 1991 or 1992. That never happened. Yet, milk prices turned out higher and Commodity Credit Corporation purchases less than had been predicted. But dairy policy is still unsettled as compared with the major crops; the industry largely agrees to wanting substantial changes but still disagrees on details.

We shall consider five areas of policy alternatives: adjustments in market support prices (grain and dairy); changes in requirements placed on farmers for program eligibility (flexibility); changes in supply management programs; changes in government outlays and means tests; and industrial policy for agriculture.

Options that move either toward or away from market orientation and increase or decrease support for farmers exist in each of those areas. I have selected options, varying in merit and demerit, that seem to have the greatest economic significance and political backing. For

99

each option, I shall set out the pros and cons and then present an analysis. It may be thought that the appropriate reference point for such analysis would be the absence of government intervention. The existing programs, however, are so long-standing and so complex that it is a major analytical undertaking to establish what prices, output, and farm income would be in the absence of the programs. I shall use USDA and Food and Agricultural Policy Research Institute baseline projections along with 1995 commodity futures prices observed in late 1994 to indicate roughly the supply-demand situation under which the 1995 farm bill will operate. I shall compare the policy options with that current-policy baseline.

Market Support Price Options

After several years of cuts in loan rates to avoid burdensome Commodity Credit Corporation stock acquisition, the levels for both wheat and corn have been gradually increased starting in 1990 (see figure 11–1). In February 1994 the USDA increased the wheat loan rate to $2.58 per bushel and corn to $1.89 per bushel for the 1994 crops. Secretary Mike Espy stated that this "demonstrates the commitment of this Administration to increase farm income which, in turn, will have a positive effect on rural areas" (USDA 1994a). The issue is how to follow up in 1995 and beyond to keep loan rates low enough that Commodity Credit Corporation stock acquisition due to loan forfeitures is nil as opposed to raising loan rates— for purposes of analysis by 5 percent.

Raising Loan Rates for Grains. Raising loan rates will not create a changed floor under *market* prices if marketing loan provisions are in effect, as they were in 1994. Under marketing loan provisions, if the market price is below the loan level, a producer can repay a Commodity Credit Corporation loan at less than the price received

100

FIGURE 11–1
SUPPORT PRICE AND FARM PRICE FOR CORN AND WHEAT

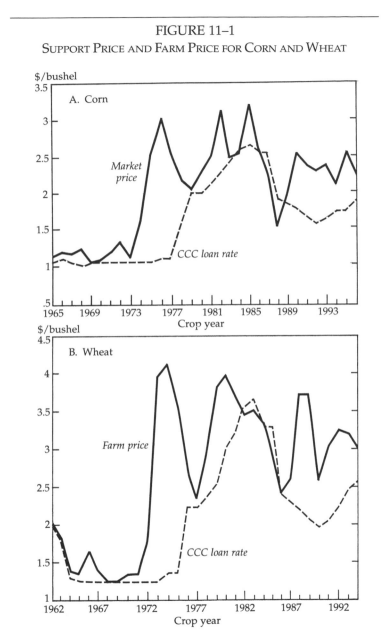

SOURCE: U.S. Department of Agriculture.

under the loan or can accept a loan deficiency payment (as in cotton) instead of obtaining a Commodity Credit Corporation loan. Under such a provision, raising loan rates affects the form and amount of payments to producers but does not affect the market price or Commodity Credit Corporation stocks. In this policy option we consider raising loan rates *without* marketing loans—we raise the effective floor under market prices.

The advantages of raising loan rates are that farmers will get larger nine-month Commodity Credit Corporation loans at favorable interest rates and will face less financial pressure to sell at harvest. In addition, farmers can sell at harvest for higher market prices in large-crop years. Finally, Commodity Credit Corporation stocks added in large-crop years will contribute to price stability through later Commodity Credit Corporation sales.

Those gains, as usual, are not costless. The disadvantages of raising loan rates are that holding prices up during the harvest season reduces seasonal consumption, for example, of feed wheat in summer, that helps utilize surplus production without government stockholding. Moreover, for every additional dollar farmers receive for their grain, buyers pay a dollar more. Finally, Commodity Credit Corporation stocks are quite costly to hold and tend to overhang the market in subsequent periods.

Analysis. With respect to farm income resulting from higher market prices for farmers—besides being offset by consumer costs—the effects of raising loan rates for grains are likely to be minor. The larger worry is the hundreds of millions of dollars that have been spent in the past holding and disposing of Commodity Credit Corporation stocks. Both the government and farmers appeared happier, and with reason, when the Commodity Credit Corporation stocks accumulated in the mid-1980s were finally drawn down in the early 1990s.

What are the chances that increases in loan rates

from current levels would generate substantial Commodity Credit Corporation stocks? Figure 11–1 shows the recent history of loan rates and market prices for wheat and corn. The graphs indicate that we have not returned to the high loan rates that caused such great difficulties in the 1960s and 1980s. But recent increases have created a situation in which a further loan rate rise would be quite risky.

Suppose the loan rates for 1995 were increased 5 percent from $2.58 to $2.71 for wheat and from $1.89 to $1.98 for corn. That would be 10 percent below the five-year average farm price for wheat and 14 percent below that average for corn. Surely that would be harmless? The answer turns on the probability that we might end up with surplus stocks at the loan levels in 1995. One way to conceptualize the risk in monetary terms is to exploit the fact that the right to sell at the Commodity Credit Corporation loan rate is equivalent, from the producer's viewpoint, to being given a put option—an option to sell the crop at a strike price equal to the loan rate. The Chicago corn price equivalent to a $1.98 price at the average farm level is about $2.20. Therefore, the premium on a put option expiring in December with a $2.20 strike price indicates roughly the value to farmers of a $1.98 loan rate for corn. As of year-end 1994, the futures price for December 1995 corn was $2.40 to $2.45 per bushel, equivalent to a U.S. average farm-level price of about $2.20. Therefore, a $1.98 loan level for 1995 corn is equivalent to a put option twenty-two cents per bushel out of the money that expires in fifteen months. Corn put options with so long to expiration are not currently traded, but the premiums on puts similarly out of the money that expire in six and eight months can be extrapolated to indicate that December 1995 puts with a $1.98 strike price would be worth about ten cents per bushel under current market expectations. With output from program participants of about eight billion bushels, the value of a

103

$1.98 loan rate is then $800 million. Thus, a seemingly innocuous increase of 5 percent in the corn loan rate gives a price floor that provides a considerable expected cost to the Treasury.

For wheat, put options corresponding to a $2.71 loan rate are further out of the money. But figure 11–1 shows that the U.S. wheat price has been at or below the *current* loan rate for three of the past ten years. So the probability that a 5 percent wheat loan rate increase would cause Commodity Credit Corporation acquisitions and market distortions is far from negligible—probably about one in three years.

In short, raising Commodity Credit Corporation loan rates would do little to solve farmers' problems while opening the door to large costs.

Dairy Price Supports. An issue in dairy policy is whether to change the support price or the method of setting its level. The arguments against an increase are parallel to those against an increase in grain loan rates. The arguments in favor are somewhat different because Commodity Credit Corporation loans are not involved. Because substantial net USDA purchases are already being made, the weight of the argument against raising the milk support price is greater than against raising loan rates for grain. The budgetary costs of raising the dairy support price are almost certain to be considerable and to substantially outweigh producers' gains because of the expanded output and reduced consumption that would be triggered.

A concrete option worth considering is to make the support price more flexible by eliminating the $10.10 floor and the requirement that the support price be increased when the USDA's projected Commodity Credit Corporation purchases are less than 3.5 billion pounds of milk equivalent and by replacing those provisions with a formula that sets the price at 85 percent of the previous five-year average manufacturing milk price, with secretarial discretion to reduce the support price by a further 10 percent. The 85 percent rule would place milk on the same footing as the grains. It would give a support price for 1994 of $10.08 per hundred pounds.

An advantage of changing dairy price supports is that the prices of dairy products would more closely reflect market conditions. In addition, Commodity Credit Corporation outlays would be reduced, and farmers would have less incentive to overinvest in milk production. Finally, USDA product donations would be more flexible.

A disadvantage of changing dairy price supports is that less product would sometimes be available for domestic and foreign food aid distribution. Moreover, if market prices fall, dairy farmers' income would decline, and there would be less seasonal stabilization of dairy prices.

Analysis. The basic procedural changes are to stop tying the support price to projected USDA purchases and to eliminate the rigid floor price of $10.10. The current procedures imply that 3.5 to 5.0 billion pounds of milk (4 to 5.5 percent of manufacturing milk use) are normally to be distributed through the USDA's domestic feeding, foreign aid, or export programs. For other commodities the government's distributive role is much more flexible—buying for school lunches, the Emergency Food Assistance Program,[1] or other purposes, as recipients' needs indicate, and using conditions in export markets to calibrate subsidized sales abroad. The same approach ought to be applied to dairy.

The more important consideration from the producers', consumers', and taxpayers' point of view is whether

---

1. That program was formerly the Temporary Emergency Food Assistance Program. "Temporary" was removed by amendment in the 1990 act (U.S. Code, 104 Stat. 3808).

the gains under the first three advantages offset the losses under the last two disadvantages. While producers have vigorously defended dairy price supports in the past, the assessments and constraints on Commodity Credit Corporation purchases in current law mean that producers do not have a great deal to lose from that option and indeed would lose nothing if government buying of milk products remained near the levels of current domestic and export programs.

Production Flexibility and Supply Management

Flexibility. The flex provisions of the 1990 legislation pertain to a farmer's use of the payment base acreage for each crop. Flex acres are important not only because of the lack of deficiency payments on the 15 percent normal flex acres, but also because on that acreage plus an additional 10 percent optional flex acres, producers may plant any crop other than fruits, vegetables, nuts, peanuts, or tobacco, or leave the acreage idle, while maintaining the payment base for future years. Thus, on 15 percent of their acreage base, producers are free to decide which program crop to plant on the basis of expected market prices rather than target prices. Moreover, a producer through zero certification can drop out of all deficiency payment programs and grow any crop desired while maintaining payment bases.

The main limitations on a farmer's flexibility to respond to market conditions are the loss of deficiency payments if another crop is planted on optional flex acres, the upper limit of flex acres to 25 percent of base acres, and the exclusion of fruits and vegetables from planting on flex acres.

Removing those three limitations would make the deficiency payment program almost completely a program of lump-sum (nondistorting) payments with respect to output reductions. A farm would receive payments based on fixed program yield and program acres, neither of which would be reduced or increased if the farmer switched to another crop in part or in full or if he changed the use of purchased inputs such as fertilizer.

With respect to output increases, however, producers could respond to increased market prices for a deficiency-payment crop only to the extent that the farm has flex acres in other program crops. Acreage reduction programs and even zero acreage reduction programs preclude a farmer participating in the program from expanding acreage of any program crop beyond the sum of acreage bases for the farm.

Also, the deficiency payment limitation of $50,000 per crop per person provides some incentive to farm in smaller rather than larger units. In corn, with a 100 bushel program yield and a seventy-five cent per bushel payment, the $50,000 limit would be reached on a base of 667 acres of corn. Under the "three-entity" rule, however, in which a person may have up to a 50 percent interest in two other farms, a farmer could receive payments on 1,333 acres. Beyond that size, payment limits impose nonnegligible obstacles for producers—loss of payments or costs of reorganization to qualify for payments. Farm operations greater than that size are atypical for grains, but payment limits are a more significant issue for cotton and rice.

In short, market orientation would be promoted by a flexibility package that retains deficiency payments for a crop, even if its flex acres are planted to another crop or idled. That package should expand flex acres from 25 percent to 100 percent of the crop acreage base. In addition, that package should allow any crop to be grown on flex acres and should allow producers to plant more than the farm's acreage base of a crop (without building the payment base) if its acreage reduction program is zero. Finally, that package should repeal payment limitations.

One advantage of a flexibility package that retains

107

deficiency payments for a crop is that it results in crop acreage determined by market conditions, not target prices, and thus increases the efficiency of agriculture. Second, such a package eliminates costs and paperwork that hinder larger operations.

A disadvantage of such a package is that nonprogram crops, notably fruits and vegetables, have to compete with subsidized farms. Moreover, more payments will go to large farms at the expense of taxpayers (or if outlays are held constant, to smaller farms).

Analysis. This issue centers on the trade-off between efficiency, in the sense of allocating resources to their best use as measured by market signals, and equity or fairness to different people. The advantages indicate that the list of changes would improve efficiency; the disadvantages are driven largely by views of fairness. But there is an efficiency aspect of the first disadvantage. If permitting fruits and vegetables on flex acres would cause fruits and vegetables to be produced more than under a complete absence of programs, then there is also an efficiency argument against that extent of flexibility. Why would this occur?

One argument is that deficiency payments would support the incomes of grain and cotton producers on the acres where they produce fruits and vegetables, so the program crop producers have an advantage *in producing fruits and vegetables* that the growers without payment bases do not have. But that would be equally true if program payments were converted to an annual lump-sum payment to historical program crop producers that was completely divorced from land except in determining the initial level.

A second argument is that deficiency payments are not fully decoupled from production, even under full flexibility as defined above, because payments do depend on the farm's remaining in production. Farmland is regularly converted to tree growing or nonagricultural activities, and even fully flexible payments would be lost when that occurs; so the payments do keep more land in production than would be the case with no programs. Under full flexibility, that would drive down the prices of program and nonprogram crops roughly proportionately. But only the owners of program crop payment bases are cushioned by deficiency payments.

Supply Management in Grains. Reforms to increase flexibility may be viewed as inconsequential tinkering as long as fifty million to sixty million acres of cropland are being held out of production under acreage reduction programs and the Conservation Reserve Program. To obtain real flexibility, the items just discussed would be supplemented with an end to acreage reduction programs and the Conservation Reserve Program.

One advantage of such a program is that it ends the social waste—the biggest component of dead-weight losses under current programs—caused by idling productive land. In addition, ending acreage reduction programs may increase farm income if demand is elastic. Finally, the program takes better advantage of increased trade opportunities under the GATT.

A disadvantage of the really flexible program is that it increases government outlays because prices fall when output increases. Moreover, ending the Conservation Reserve Program payments reduces farm income. Finally, annual acreage reduction programs have become the government's primary tool for year-to-year commodity market stabilization; ending acreage reduction programs would make prices more variable.

Analysis. We can estimate the costs and benefits of acreage reduction programs and the Conservation Reserve Program in several ways. All are conjectural as they require judgment of what producers would do in the ab-

109

sence of acreage reduction programs. Fortunately, the experience of zero acreage reduction programs for all the grains in 1994 provides some direct evidence. Consider what the wheat markets would look like in 1996 if zero acreage reduction programs were continued.[2]

The mid-1994 Food and Agricultural Policy Research Institute baseline acreage reduction program for a continuation of current wheat policy is 5 percent for 1996 (indeed for each crop from 1995 through 2002). Moving to a zero acreage reduction program would add three million acres to crop production. Under flexibility that acreage may not all go back to wheat, but for maximum effect suppose it does. At 90 percent of the U.S. baseline yield (because acreage reduction program land should not be the best land), those acres would produce 105 million bushels of wheat. That is 4.1 percent of baseline consumption. With an elasticity of demand for all wheat (domestic use and export) of -1.1, the market price of wheat would fall by 3.7 percent, or eleven cents per bushel.

The effects of a 3.7 percent decline in the price of wheat at baseline quantities include the government costs of higher payments—$200 million on 1,800 payment bushels and $80 million on formerly idled acres. In addition, the government savings on export sales (the export enhancement program equivalent)[3] are $138 million on 1,250 bushels of exports. The consumer savings

2. Large amounts of Conservation Reserve Program acreage would not be returned to production until 1997 in any case.

3. The reduction in price of exported wheat is scored as a savings of government expenditures because about $1 billion annually is now spent on export enhancement program subsidies to sell wheat at lower prices abroad. Relaxing acreage reduction programs means that export enhancement can be accomplished without government costs. Of course, if we were analyzing the elimination of both acreage reduction programs *and* the export enhancement program, we could not count that gain.

from lower prices on 1,250 bushels of domestic consumption are $138 million. Farm incomes suffer a $275 million loss on production. Farmers do, however, receive an extra payment on base production of $200 million and an $85 per acre return over variable cost on three million acres of $255 million. Thus, the farmers gain $180 million. In total, the United States gains $135 million from the 3.7 percent decline in the price of wheat at baseline quantities.

Over the longer term, if we similarly analyze bringing 10.6 million acres of wheat base out of the Conservation Reserve Program, we would have 371 million additional bushels. Ending both the Conservation Reserve Program and 5 percent wheat acreage reduction programs would increase U.S. wheat available by 14 percent (using the Food and Agricultural Policy Research Institute's baseline values for 1998). With a longer-term elasticity of demand for wheat of -2, the market price would fall 7 percent or twenty cents per bushel. In this case the costs and benefits include saved Conservation Reserve Program payments of $480 million, higher deficiency payments of $-$360$ million, the export enhancement program equivalent of $260 million, and farm income of $115, for a total gain of $775 million.

The net benefits to farmers, consumers, the government budget, and the nation as a whole are greater in the longer run because of the higher elasticity of demand. That reflects the fact that over the longer term, the main effect of acreage reduction programs is to give away export markets to foreign producers.[4]

---

4. What about the argument that the United States, as a large factor in world grain markets, can exercise monopoly power by cutting production and exporting less? There would in fact be net gains to producers from a precisely chosen production cutback, *if* farmers are free to redeploy their land to other crops. But production control through acreage reduction programs requires land idling, and that dissipates much of farmers' gains from higher prices.

Those calculations omit the pervasive uncertainty in grain markets. What weight shall we give to the disadvantage that ending acreage reduction programs destabilizes prices? The consumer benefit arises when, as occurred following the short crop of 1993, the corn or wheat acreage reduction percentage is decreased when corn stocks become low enough. In that respect acreage reduction programs are a substitute for larger carryover stocks. In the absence of acreage reduction programs triggered by stock levels, private grain merchants and farmers would have a greater incentive to hold stocks in lean years. In 1993 the market let stocks decline in part because everyone knew that lower acreage reduction programs in 1994 would increase 1994 production. If acreage reduction programs had already been zero in 1993, there would have been more reason to hold carryover stocks against the chance of another short crop in 1994. In short, it is not clear that a policy supporting an acreage reduction program is a better way to stabilize price than relying on stockholding. And, if private stockholding provides insufficient price stabilization, it is likely to be more efficient to subsidize stockholding through a much-simplified version of the farmer-owned reserve program than to manipulate acreage reduction programs.

Supply Management in Dairy. Governmental attempts to control milk production have been less systematic than for the grains and are still unsettled. In the 1990 act Congress expressed a general sense that USDA dairy product inventories should be controlled through policy measures beyond the price support scheme summarized earlier. Because of disagreements within the dairy industry, however, no particular plan was adopted. Instead, the secretary of agriculture was instructed to submit recommendations by August 1, 1991—eight months after the 1990 act became law—for policies that would limit USDA purchases to six billion pounds annually.

In the 1980s the government tried two approaches. From 1984 through 1985, producers had been offered diversion payments if they agreed to reduce their output 5 to 15 percent below previous production levels. That program paid producers almost $1 billion, but its effectiveness was reduced because the program appealed primarily to producers who by accident or design were already on track to produce less. Commodity Credit Corporation net removals were indeed reduced in 1984 and 1985, before the support price reductions of 1985. But the effect was only temporary.

In the 1985 act Congress made a more ambitious effort through the dairy herd termination program. Under that program producers bid to retire their entire herd and remain out of dairy farming for at least five years. That program paid $1.9 billion in fiscal years 1986 through 1988, of which about $700 million were financed through a levy on farmers who continued to produce. The program resulted in the slaughter of an estimated one million cows (8 percent of the cow population), with their number declining from 11.1 million in 1986 to 10.3 million in 1988. But the upward march of milk production continued, and cow numbers by the end of the 1980s appeared essentially on the slow downward trend they had followed since 1970 (see figure 11–2).

In the 1990 act the secretary of agriculture was instructed not to consider either of two "prohibited programs" in his supply management study: reductions in the milk support price or any dairy herd termination program (U.S. Code, 104 Stat. 3376). The latter prohibition reflected not only the questionable effectiveness of the 1986 through 1988 program, but also the strong opposition of beef producers, who believed dairymen were being subsidized to dump cow beef in their unsubsidized market.

In 1991 Secretary Edward R. Madigan in due course sent Congress his report but found no desirable supply

113

FIGURE 11–2
MILK PRODUCTION AND NUMBER OF COWS, 1970–1992

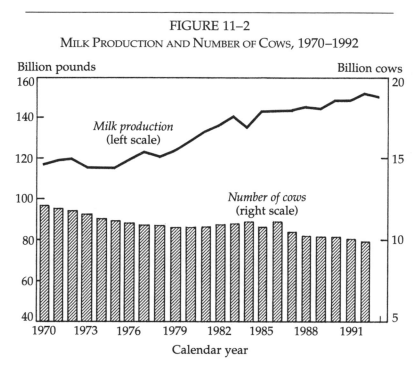

SOURCE: U.S. Department of Agriculture.

control program. With the dairy industry still unable to agree, Congress did nothing in 1991, and supply management remains an open issue. We still have assessments of about 1 percent of the price of milk on producers who expand milk production, but that is the only element of supply control.

The dairy industry has remained largely convinced that some supply management scheme is needed. Led by the National Milk Producers' Federation, a coalition of cooperatives and producers groups has endorsed a self-help approach to manage supplies (Barr 1993). That would combine elements of previous programs, notably assessments on producers to finance a range of price-enhancing activities. An industry board would make key decisions about the program. Analytically, the coalition

114

proposes to establish a governmentally sanctioned cartel for dairy products.[5] The powers of the board vary in alternative self-help proposals. As described in Barr (1993), the dairy stabilization board would have the following features and powers. It would be authorized to intervene in dairy product markets at prices higher than Commodity Credit Corporation support prices. It would be funded by assessments of up to twenty cents per hundredweight on milk sold by producers. That funding is intended to be sufficient to buy up to two billion pounds of milk equivalent, in years when Commodity Credit Corporation removals, absent the board's purchases, are projected to be between five billion and seven billion pounds of milk equivalent (as is the case for 1995). The board's purchased products would be sold in domestic or foreign markets chosen by the board to be least competitive with normal commercial outlets. If Commodity Credit Corporation removals are projected to exceed seven billion pounds, producer assessments, as under current law, would be used to make further purchases by the board. If the price of manufacturing milk fell to within fifty cents per hundredweight of the support price for two consecutive months, the board would collect a further excess marketing assessment to control production.

One advantage of such a proposal is that it supports dairy producers without increasing federal budget outlays. Second, it gives producers a role in shaping their own program.

A disadvantage of the program is that it is costly to consumers of dairy products. In addition, the program places the burden of adjustment on producers who

5. The milk marketing order system has itself been characterized as a cartel, but a cartel with free entry. The self-help plans would, under some proposals, set up a cartel in more nearly the classic sense of an arrangement among producers to restrain output placed on the market (like the Organization of Petroleum Exporting Countries, the International Coffee Agreement, or the U.S. peanut program).

would otherwise increase production and who tend to be lower-cost producers.

Analysis. The self-help cartel would be difficult to implement because of the divergence of interests among producers, which indeed has so far scuttled industry-wide agreement on any plan. An underlying problem is that, in the West and Southeast particularly, some producers can profitably expand at current prices. But others, particularly in the upper Midwest and Northeast, are economically pressed and need higher prices for long-term survival. Those disagreements probably preclude any plan that would be very costly to consumers or beneficial to producers.

There is a more fundamental problem with the approach. The proposed program is not just accelerating socialism when it is elsewhere in retreat; it is socialism that hands over the relevant governmental monopoly powers and agencies to a private industry. It is hard to imagine a worse precedent for economic policy making.

Budget Savings Options

Some farm interests are gloomy, and in agribusiness, too, there is concern about how to get the public to continue parting with its money at current rates. Both the 1985 and 1990 farm legislation contained measures to reduce federal budget outlays for agricultural programs, as reviewed earlier. The most significant steps were cutting target prices in 1985 and eliminating deficiency payments on 15 percent of each farmer's payment acreage base in 1990. Those changes affect only the crops that receive deficiency payments—wheat, rice, corn, barley, sorghum, oats, and cotton. Milk has also been subject to support price reductions, beginning in 1982. Milk and nonpayment crops such as sugar, peanuts, and tobacco have been subject to assessments, albeit amounting to only 1 or 2 percent of the commodity's value. The Clinton administration has shown interest in further cuts. As a presidential candidate in 1992, Bill Clinton proposed eliminating the honey program. Congress has followed that recommendation. The fiscal year 1994 appropriations act, signed in September 1993, cut subsidy payments and the value of Commodity Credit Corporation purchases to zero and made the honey program essentially an ordinary ("recourse") loan program with no capability to provide a price floor. In addition, Congress cut fiscal year 1994 appropriations for wool 25 percent and scheduled them for a phaseout by the end of 1995.

Yet federal outlays for agricultural commodity support have not yet fallen below the 1990 baseline. The cuts and assessments have been offset by increases due to commodity price changes, disaster payments, and expanded export promotion programs (see table 10–2).

Further proposals for reduced budget outlays are inevitable, although the agricultural committees will probably not initiate them. Even the agriculture committees may have to face up to a budget problem caused by the expiration of the Conservation Reserve Program. Conservation Reserve Program spending goes to zero as currently existing contracts are phased out between 1995 and 2002. Therefore, even maintaining the Conservation Reserve Program, by renewing contracts as they expire, should be counted as a new outlay for budget-scoring purposes. Thus, continuing the Conservation Reserve Program, a high priority for many environmental as well as farm groups, would require cutting some existing programs. That is the CBO's interpretation, but the OMB, in its mid-1994 budget review, switched its baseline to include spending on the Conservation Reserve Program's thirty-eight million acres.

I shall consider two broad approaches to cutting commodity outlays: means-testing payments and across-the-board cuts.

Means-testing Payments. Current law limits deficiency payments to $50,000, continuing a practice that was in-

117

troduced along with the target-price approach in the Agricultural Act of 1970. In 1970 the limitation, at $55,000 per farmer per commodity, was estimated to affect about 1,100 farmers, almost entirely in cotton, and to have reduced payments by $58 million out of a $3.5 billion total (Halcrow 1977, 193). The estimated budget savings are small, compared with total outlays, but amount to $53,000 annually per affected farm. Thus, it was from the beginning worthwhile for farmers to try to become smaller for deficiency payment purposes.

Subsequent farm bills have specified separate payment limits for disaster programs ($100,000), loan deficiency payments ($75,000), the honey, wool, and mohair programs ($200,000 each), Conservation Reserve payments ($50,000), and combined deficiency, disaster, and other payments ($250,000), as well as tightening the definition of who qualifies as a person for payment purposes and limiting the number of payment-receiving enterprises a farmer may participate in owning. Analysts estimate that the current three-entity rule, discussed earlier, in conjunction with the other limitations reduces payments by $70 million annually (as of 1989) compared with the situation with no payment limits.

In the 1990 farm bill debate, urban congressional representatives introduced amendments to restrict payments further by not permitting any payments to farmers who, for example, had more than $1 million annually in sales. The amendment of that type that received the widest publicity and was debated in the full House was one that would have prohibited payments to anyone who had off-farm income of over $100,000. The idea was to get a wedge in the door of payment reform by excluding doctors, lawyers, and wealthy businessmen. About 60 percent of those voting in the House voted against that amendment, however.

In its budget submissions to Congress, the Clinton

administration has followed the Bush administration in endorsing the general idea of means testing. The Bush administration's 1992 budget submission claimed that "deficiency payments have gone to more than 10,000 individuals whose annual adjusted gross income from non-farming sources has exceeded $125,000" and estimated that they received about $90 million in payments. The administration suggested a means test to make those people ineligible for farm program payments (U.S. Budget 1992, 139). The Clinton administration included a broader proposal in its 1993 budget to make anyone having over a $100,000 adjusted gross income from all sources on his tax returns ineligible for payments. That was estimated to save $140 million annually when fully implemented. The CBO, however, estimates that such a measure would save $60 million annually (CBO 1994, 215).

Considering either the $100,000 adjusted gross income test or the $1 million sales test as a policy option, the advantages and disadvantages are similar. The advantages of the means test are that it saves government outlays, that losers do not need the payments, and that it opens the door politically for further reform. The disadvantages are that such a test induces resource expenditure to avoid losing payments, penalizes farming enterprises that may be relatively efficient, and reduces the ability of acreage reduction programs to control production.

Analysis. We can expect the actual savings from means testing to be much smaller than figures such as the $140 million above would suggest, because it is too easy to convert payments into roughly equivalent market returns. The lawyer who owns a farm only has to rent the cropland out to a "real" farmer, who will then be the farmer of record for USDA purposes. The market rental value of the farm will include the value of payments that

119

the renter can expect to receive, so that the lawyer can retain the value of the payments by, in effect, selling them to someone else.

It is costly to make those arrangements, which are revealed as not preferred by the lawyer, since by hypothesis they were not made until induced by the means test. The cost has to be counted as a dead-weight loss of the means test.

The penalty for relatively efficient farmers could be important, particularly for means testing based on sales. The USDA estimates that 16,000 farms, .8 percent of all U.S. farms, sold products valued at $1,000,000 or more in 1991. Those farms received $443 million in government payments, which were 5.4 percent of all payments in 1991, received an average of $27,000, and had an average net cash income of $1.2 million as estimated by the USDA (1993a, 69).[6]

Thus, the USDA could hope to reduce its outlays by 5 percent, if that is required in total budget reduction efforts, just by denying payments to farms with over $1 million in sales. The owners typically are well-off. Moreover, the payments average only about 2 percent of their $1 + million net incomes.

Such a scheme has problems, however. First, the USDA is not well equipped to determine, when a farmer signs up for program participation, what the farm's sales are. The USDA could require income tax returns if legislation permitted, but a USDA farm is not the unit of account for income tax purposes, so it is not clear that the data provided would still apply. In addition, such a scheme will induce the indirect capture of payments through rental or other contracting, as discussed above. Note also that while the farms with $1 million in sales get 5.4 percent of all payments, they sell 10.5 percent of commodities receiving payments. For all farms the gov-

---

6. IRS adjusted gross income would be less.

ernment paid $8.2 billion on $28.4 billion of payment-receiving commodities in 1991; payments were 29 percent of the value of those commodities (grains and cotton). But for the farms with $1 million in sales, the government paid $443 million on $3.0 billion of payment-receiving commodities; payments on the large farms were 15 percent of the value of the commodities. Thus, the large farms have already been driven out of programs to a substantial extent by existing payment limits, or else they have already found ways to capture payments indirectly.

Suppose that existing payment limits really have been effective and that farms with $1 million in sales have been driven out of programs to the extent indicated. That would mean that those farms get 20 percent less for program crops than smaller farms do. Removing payments completely from the largest farms would mean that their effective price for program crops is about 35 percent less than the price farms with less than $250,000 in sales receive. Since the number of large farms is growing and smaller ones shrinking, it is likely that the large ones are lower-cost producers. A strict limitation on program benefits to larger farms thus subsidizes high-cost relative to low-cost producers by causing large farms to receive perhaps 20 percent less per unit output than small farms. Means tests may have appeal if we see farm programs as welfare programs, but they are perverse for farm programs as industrial policy.

Crittenden (1993, 207) cites some of those distributional facts and recognizes that full means testing is not imminent. "In the meantime," she helpfully suggests, "all recipients should be obliged to tithe a portion of their production to programs to feed the poor." Even for the longer term there appears to be no easily attainable alternative budget strategy to across-the-board cuts in farm program spending.

Across-the-Board Cuts. Across-the-board reductions will have to come predominantly from deficiency payments, since that is where most of the spending is. The main alternatives are cuts in target prices, as in the 1985 act, or reductions in payment acreage, as in 1990. Which of those approaches is preferable? If payments were strictly lump sum—determined by a payment rate and quantity on which payments were absolutely fixed—then the choice would not matter. With respect to the chief way in which current law does affect producer behavior— imperfect flexibility among crops—cutbacks in payment acreage reduce the distortive effects more. That increases planting flexibility by increasing normal flex acres. But cutting target prices helps, too, by reducing the incentive to make acreage decisions based on expected deficiency payments.

A consideration that may be more important is the role of price variability. A ten-cent reduction in the market price can fully offset the budget savings from a ten-cent reduction in a target price. But an equal budget savings from a cut in payment acreage would not be so vulnerable to a market price decline. Consider a specific example, corn. Suppose we want to score a 50 percent reduction in corn deficiency payments in 1996. The current-policy baseline has a corn target price of $2.75 per bushel, a market price of $2.15 per bushel, and payment bushels of 5.1 billion. Therefore, baseline corn program spending is $3.06 billion, and we need to save $1.53 billion. The government can accomplish that in two ways: by cutting the target price thirty cents per bushel or by cutting payment acres by 50 percent, which would mean increasing the 15 percent nonpayment base to about 55 percent.

If events turn out as projected in the baseline, then the $1.53 billion are duly saved under either alternative. But the market price is quite uncertain. If it turns out to be $1.85, under the option of cutting the target price, outlays will be $3.06 billion, and the savings will be zero.

FIGURE 11-3
BUDGET SAVINGS BY CUTTING PAYMENT ACRES OR
TARGET PRICES FOR CORN

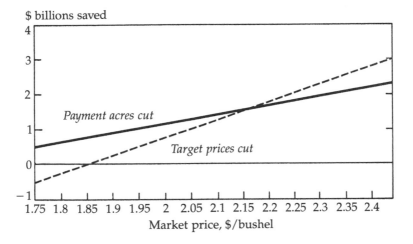

Under the option of cutting payment acres, outlays will be $2.3 billion, and the savings will be $760 million. So the savings are less at risk under the second option. Of course, if prices are higher than the baseline level, the first option offers additional savings. Figure 11-3 summarizes the possibilities. The expected value of the savings is the same for both options, but the government incurs less risk in the payment acreage reduction. Farmers face more risk, however. Since farm programs are particularly valuable to farmers when prices are unexpectedly low, cutting target prices may be preferable to cutting payment acres to achieve at least some of the desired budgetary savings.

To analyze a concrete option, consider cutting target prices by 15 percent and payment acres by 10 percent over five years. Starting in 1996, target prices would be cut by 3 percent each year and payment acreage by 2 percent. One advantage of such a policy is that it would substantially reduce government spending. Another advantage is that farmers would gear production more to market realities. The disadvantage is that farm income would decline.

Analysis. That policy option involves a classic trade-off between the general public and a producer interest group. The chief economic question is how much the general public will gain relative to what farmers lose—the recoverable dead-weight losses caused by current policies.

Consider such an option for wheat after full implementation in the year 2000. The target price will be $3.40 and payment acres about fifty million. Averaging USDA and Food and Agricultural Policy Research Institute baselines, the expected market price of wheat is about $3.10 per bushel in 2000. Keeping payment yields at thirty-four bushels per acre, deficiency payments would be $510 million, compared with about $1.7 billion under current law. That cuts outlays by $1.2 billion or 70 percent from the current-law baseline.

The question can be raised whether the wheat price would remain at the $3.10 baseline price under the deficiency payment cuts. The Food and Agricultural Policy Research Institute baseline assumes a 5 percent wheat acreage reduction program in 2000, although the USDA baseline has a zero acreage reduction program. Supposing the 5 percent estimate is correct, one needs to consider whether program participation pays when deficiency payments have been reduced so far. If producers drop out to produce on acreage reduction program land, their added output will depress market prices.

Consider a person with 100 acres of wheat base. Under the year 2000 program parameters, payments would be received on seventy acres, with twenty-five normal flex acres and five acreage reduction program acres receiving no payments. With a payment yield of thirty-four bushels per acre—the U.S. average—the producer receives a deficiency payment of $714. If he drops out of the program, he could plant the five acreage reduction program acres and he would have more options for the twenty-five flex acres. The gains on the twenty-five acres are likely to be minimal, given the ability to plant any program crop while a wheat program participant. But the gains on the acreage reduction program land may be considerable. If net returns or rental value were zero when idled under the acreage reduction program and $60 per acre when cropped—the Food and Agricultural Policy Research Institute's projection of nonparticipants' net returns per acre in 2000—then the producer gains $300 by dropping out. But since he gives up $714 in payments, it pays to keep participating. Therefore, I assume that there are enough participants to make the 5 percent acreage reduction program as effective as in the Food and Agricultural Policy Research Institute's baseline and that the baseline market prices are still appropriate.

There might be substantial adjustments on flex acres if only the wheat program were changed, but with all commodities' target prices and payment acres being cut, that is less likely.

I show comparable results of such a policy option for corn, cotton, and rice in table 11–1. For cotton and corn, the Food and Agricultural Policy Research Institute's baseline acreage reduction programs, 7.5 percent and 12.5 percent, are larger, and one would expect a significant reduction in participation with a large decline in deficiency payments. Consequently, market prices under the policy reforms are slightly lower than in the current policy baseline. Even with lower market prices, budget savings are considerable.

Rice, however, gets off relatively lightly because current law gives a target price so far above the market price that cutting the target price 15 percent only cuts the payment rate about 25 percent. In comparison, cutting the target price cuts the wheat payment rate 67 percent, corn

TABLE 11–1

USDA Baseline Spending under Current Law
and after Reform[a]

	Corn		Cotton		Rice	
	Current law	After cuts	Current law	After cuts	Current law	After cuts
Target price ($/bushel)	2.75	2.35	.729	.62	10.71	9.62
Market price ($/bushel)	2.25	2.20	.57	.55	6.60	6.60
Program yield (bushels/acre)	104	104	600	600	48.55	48.55
Payment acres (millions)	58	51	8	7	2.5	2.2
Deficiency payments ($ billions)	3.0	.8	.8	.3	.5	.3
Savings from reform ($ billions)		2.2		.5		.2

a. Target prices cut 15 percent; payment acres reduced by 10 percent of base.

70 percent, and cotton 55 percent. Payment acreage cuts of 10 percent of base, however, have about the same percentage effect on government spending for all crops. Thus, program acreage cuts are more equitable across commodities than equal-percentage target price cuts.

For all the commodities considered, payments by the year 2000 would be reduced from baseline levels by $1.2 billion for wheat, $2.2 billion for corn (to which we should add $.4 billion for other feed grains), and $.3 billion each for cotton and rice. The annual budget savings would total $4.4 billion for the deficiency-payment crops. That is a reduction of two-thirds from the $6.6 billion current-law baseline for the crops used in this analysis.

The objection to that policy option is the loss of payments by the farmers who would otherwise receive them. Because of increased ability to plant the most profitable crops and the removal of acreage reduction

program constraints for farmers who no longer participate, however, farmers would recoup some of that loss.
In a more detailed study of the deficiency payment programs, Lin estimated that from 1984 through 1987 farm
income increased $.70 for each dollar spent on deficiency
payments (Lin 1989, 16). That would imply that landowners would get back 30 percent or $1.3 billion of the
$4.4 billion payments lost, for a net loss of $3.1 billion, of
which about 70 percent ($2.2 billion) would be borne by
farm operators.

Commodity producers would naturally object to
that loss. In the political arena that loss may well count
for more than the taxpayers' $6.0 billion gains.[7] It is dan-
gerous for farmers and costly to the economy, however,
to have the matter turn simply on political clout. And
many farmers do not want (and most do not need) farm
programs as just a variety of welfare payment. An issue
economists might helpfully address is how to structure
agricultural policy in such a way as to assist agriculture
while making the economy more efficient rather than
creating dead-weight losses. That leads to a broader set
of policy options that I shall discuss under the heading
of industrial policy.

Industrial Policy for Agriculture

The analytical approach to policy options that go beyond
redistributing income is to consider areas in which gov-

---

7. The difference between the farmers' loss and the taxpayers'
gain, the marginal dead-weight loss of the deficiency payment programs, is actually greater than the $1.3 billion cited. The reason is that
reducing outlays by $4.4 billion is worth more than $4.4 billion because of dead-weight losses involved in taxation to raise those funds.
Alston and Hurd (1990) argue for a range whose midpoint is thirty-
five cents per dollar raised. Then the total gains to the U.S. economy
of the $4.4 billion cuts would be $2.9 billion. Landowners give up $3.1
billion, and the rest of the economy gains $6.0 billion. In addition,
that accounting omits administrative costs of the program, currently
about $800 million annually for the Commodity Credit Corporation
programs.

ernment action can plausibly improve on the workings of the market. Those areas include environmental externalities, price stabilization, public good aspects of new knowledge and information, and dealing with other nations whose policies affect U.S. exports.

One reason the 1990 farm act was larger than its predecessors is that it included a wide range of programs that go beyond the traditional commodity policies. Congress intended many of them to conserve resources or to improve the environment. More broadly, such a policy agenda constitutes industrial policy for agriculture— regulations and public investment intended to influence production decisions in the sector. The purpose may be to increase the profitability of farming or to generate broader social benefits from agriculture—the same purposes as traditional commodity programs but using different policy instruments. There is often, however, a sense that broader social purposes play a larger role in industrial policy.

In table 11–2 I list many such programs included in the 1990 act. With the Clinton administration dedicated to public investment generally, and with an even wider regulatory agenda, what are we likely to see in the 1995 farm bill? The possibilities appear endless, but two facts should be noted. First, many of the 1990 act programs have been implemented only minimally or not at all because of a lack of funds appropriated to carry them out.[8] Second, after two years, the Clinton administration's environmental regulatory actions do not appear to be so sweeping as had been expected. Although the administration proposed grazing fee increases and environmen-

---

8. In June 1994 the OMB published a final rule implementing the Farmland Protection Policy Act, part of the 1981 farm bill. So the lack of action to date on 1990 act programs does not mean that they will never be implemented. (See "After 13 Years, Farmland Act Crawls to Finish Line," *Washington Post*, July 5, 1994.)

TABLE 11–2

INDUSTRIAL POLICY IN FOOD, AGRICULTURE, CONSERVATION, AND TRADE ACT OF 1990

Title XIV. Conservation
  Section 1438. Wetlands reserve program
  Section 1439. Agricultural water quality incentives
  Section 1440. Environmental easement program
  Section 1441. Tree planting initiative
  Section 1451. Integrated farm management program
  Sections 1465–1470. Farmland protection
  Section 1491. Pesticide recordkeeping

Title XVI. Research
  Sections 1619–1629. Sustainable agriculture research and education
  Sections 1632–1635. National genetics resources program
  Sections 1657–1664. Alternative agricultural research and commercialization
  Section 1668. Biotechnology risk assessment
  Section 1671. Plant genome mapping program
  Section 1676. Turkey research center
  Section 1680. Assistive technology program for farmers with disabilities

Title XIX. Agricultural Promotion
  Sections 1905–1918. Pecans
  Sections 1921–1933. Mushrooms
  (similar separate programs for potatoes, limes, soybeans, honey, wool, cotton, fluid milk in sections 1935–1999R

Title XX. Grain Quality

Title XXI. Organic Certification

Title XXIV. Global Climate Change

SOURCE: U.S. Code, 104 Stat. 3359–3674, table of contents.

tal requirements for grazing livestock on public lands in the winter of 1993, dramatic changes now appear unlikely to occur. The most significant environmental legislation of 1994, the Clean Drinking Water Act as passed in the Senate in May, actually weakens the requirements on cities for testing water supplies. The Endangered Species

Act, the Clean Water Act, and the Federal Fungicide, Insecticide, and Rodenticide Act, all of which were thought to pose a regulatory threat to agriculture in reauthorization during 1993 and 1994, now seem as likely to reduce regulatory requirements as to increase them—and not until 1995 or 1996 in any case—especially with Republican majorities in Congress.

Nonetheless, we can expect the 1995 farm bill to consider a wide range of programs of public investment in research, environmental improvement, and promotion of new uses for agricultural products. Environmental, conservation, and research options are the subject of other monographs in the AEI Studies in Agricultural Policy. I shall only briefly discuss public spending on research and promotion with emphasis on new uses of farm products. I shall state the policy option in the spirit of the pay-as-you-go requirement of the 1990 and 1993 budget agreements.

Reallocate Government Spending from Commodity Price Support to Research and Promotion of New Uses for Farm Products. The advantages of such an option are that it confers benefits on consumers and the environment as well as on farmers and that it generates less dead-weight loss since instead of idling land, it creates uses for the products of it. One disadvantage of the public investment option is that farmers may not gain so much from a given level of spending on research and promotion as they do from commodity programs such as deficiency payments. In addition, such a policy option generates more dead-weight losses due to "pork" in research and promotion programs.

Analysis. The argument in favor of the public investment approach is essentially that it does better than commodity programs in a benefit-cost test. Indeed, a large body of literature estimates that the social rate of return to research is greater than the rate of return to investment in the economy generally. Some have questioned that finding. But while the evidence is not incontrovertible, the weight of it today indicates that research has increased agricultural productivity sufficiently to more than repay the costs.

What is much less clear is whether farmers gain as much from, say, $1 billion in research as compared with $1 billion in deficiency payments. In neither case will farmers get all the benefits, because of dead-weight losses and sharing the gains with other interested parties such as farm input suppliers and marketing firms. For the wheat and corn programs from 1984 through 1987, Lin (1989, 16) estimates that producers gained about seventy cents per dollar spent by the federal government.

Estimates are lacking of farmers' benefits from federal research spending. For state-level research and research in smaller countries like New Zealand and Australia, one can more convincingly make the case that farmers gain. The reason is that benefits from reductions in production costs must largely go to producers because international or national markets set product prices. But for a large country like the United States, increases in output at reduced costs are likely to benefit consumers more than producers and may not benefit producers at all if product demand is inelastic. Thus, some U.S. milk producers are suspicious of the growth hormone BST. Over the long term and given the importance of world markets even for U.S. farm products, however, it seems likely that farmers benefit. Urban and rural interests are more likely to agree on public investment in research than in commodity programs because research generates gains to society as a whole. The terms of debate are quite different for commodity programs than for research programs. With commodity programs it is accepted that farmers gain, and the question is what is in it for consumers and taxpayers. With research it is accepted that

131

consumers and taxpayers gain, and the question is what is in it for farmers.

The discussion so far has not involved industrial policy in the sense of governmental direction of research spending details. The 1990 farm act, with the titles listed in table 11–2, moved in that direction. The alternative is to let the scientific community, traditionally through the land-grant universities and the USDA's Agricultural Research Service, decide how to allocate research efforts. The argument for more congressional micromanagement is that the USDA and the universities are not sufficiently interested in practical, profit-generating research, but instead are too much focused on scientific disciplinary research with little commercial value. The argument against congressional industrial policy is that Congress does not know what the promising lines of research are, in terms of either pure science or commercial prospects, and will end up mainly distributing pork to the scientific enterprises whose snouts are most deeply in the trough.

With respect to federal spending on commodity promotion, the arguments are weaker for both the benefits of the programs and the desirability of detailed industrial policy from Congress. Such evidence as exists for benefits of promotion programs usually indicates that the programs generate returns for producers that cover their costs. But there is doubt about the persistence of demand increases, and generally the evidence is weaker than for research programs.

The area of industrial policy in which those issues appear most concretely is the development and promotion of new uses for farm-produced products. While the monograph by Julian M. Alston and Philip G. Pardey, *Making Science Pay: The Economics of Agricultural R&D Policy*, in the AEI Studies in Agricultural Policy demonstrates that publicly funded research is as political as commodity programs, congressional encouragement of publicly funded research is inherently attractive if the alternative is less research spending and we believe that research in general is likely to be a socially productive investment. Why not go a step further and specifically direct spending on new uses that have environmental benefits? One such benefit is cleaner air from vehicle fuels that produce fewer harmful emissions. The Clean Air Act Amendments of 1990 recognized that oxygenates in gasoline cause cleaner burning. Ethanol (alcohol) and its esterized product ETBE are useful oxygenates for that purpose. The Clean Air Act requires oxygenated fuel in many cities during seasons when smog is a problem. The existence of environmental benefits has been challenged, however, on the ground that oxygenates increase emissions of formaldehyde and acetaldehyde, which are carcinogens.[9] Moreover, ethanol is not the only oxygenate additive available; methanol (wood alcohol) and its derivative MTBE also work. Indeed, the gasoline companies in general prefer methanol because it is cheaper and more easily handled. But methanol is made primarily from natural gas, while ethanol is made primarily from corn (in the United States). Ethanol is on the front line of "new uses" of farm products; it already uses about 350 million bushels of corn annually.

The implementation of the Clean Air Act Amendments is industrial policy par excellence. A complex choice has to be made, where pollution externalities are involved, along with new technology. Because of the externalities, even competitive markets may fail to allocate resources to maximize social benefits. Implementing of the Clean Air Act Amendments has become predominantly a political struggle between those with economic interests in ethanol versus those with economic interests in methanol.

The issue is further complicated because each gallon of ethanol is subsidized, through tax reductions, at a rate

---

9. See letter from "Oxy-Busters," *New York Times*, October 1, 1994.

of fifty-four cents per gallon. Thus, to pass a cost-benefit test, ethanol fuels must generate environmental or other public benefits that exceed those of methanol by fifty-four cents per gallon. The best prospect for such gains is to plant corn in cropland that would be idled in acreage reduction programs under baseline policies.

The Food and Agricultural Policy Research Institute's baseline for 2000 estimates the returns to growing corn at market prices rather than leaving land idle at $139 per acre. For each acre of land used to grow corn for ethanol, trend yields generate 332 gallons of ethanol. The subsidy of fifty-four cents per gallon then costs $179. The losses exceed the gains by $40 per acre. That represents twelve cents per gallon of ethanol, or 1.2 cents per gallon of gasohol (about 10 percent ethanol). Therefore, if ethanol-based gasohol has 1.2 cents per gallon in environmental benefits over its unsubsidized competitors, switching at the margin from other oxygenates to ethanol while decreasing acreage reduction programs breaks even on the social account and increases farm income by generating returns to farmers on formerly idled acres.

Given a 5 percent baseline acreage reduction program in the year 2000, about three million acres could be moved into corn for ethanol. That would generate about one billion gallons of ethanol (equivalent to about .67 percent of U.S. gasoline consumption). The added subsidy cost would be $540 million.[10] The added farm income would be $417 million. Thus, added ethanol production generates farm income with about the same efficiency as deficiency payments (seventy-seven cents in farm income per dollar of government cost). But with the ethanol subsidy we also get some clean air benefits.[11]

---

10. Note that this is *not* in the USDA budget but comes from funds that would otherwise go to transportation programs.

11. What about the gains of ethanol manufacturers, such as Archer-Daniel-Midlands? They gain to the extent that they can produce ethanol for less than the subsidized price. It seems quite likely

Thus, while corn-based ethanol may be "one of the greatest energy boondoggles ever conceived" (*Wall Street Journal*, October 3, 1994), it is not conspicuously profligate in the context of existing farm commodity programs.

Some might also consider the Conservation Reserve Program a part of industrial policy that generates farm income benefits at relatively low dead-weight loss, while providing environmental benefits. The cost effectiveness of the Conservation Reserve Program has also been questioned, however. Walter N. Thurman's monograph, *Assessing the Environmental Impact of Farm Policies*, in the AEI Studies in Agricultural Policy provides a detailed discussion.

Analysts properly consider several agricultural trade policy options as elements of industrial policy. The most costly items are export subsidy programs for wheat, dairy products, and other commodities. More attuned to the regulatory and "picking winners" aspects of industrial policy are the market promotion program with an emphasis on high-value exports and policies like the "circle of poison" restrictions on pesticide exports. Columnist George Will called a recent budget reduction in the market promotion program "a 13.6 percent cut in a program that is 100 percent indefensible" and called its supplements to advertising activities abroad "ineffective welfare payments to corporations" (*Washington Post*, July 11, 1993). Is the criticism fair? A policy step that would have trivial costs but could contribute greatly to sensible industrial policy is establishing a continuing unit for benefit-cost assessment of regulatory proposals and public investments affecting agriculture. Such assessments would likely recommend completely eliminating the ex-

that in 2000, efficient ethanol producers would need only thirty to forty cents in subsidy to be competitive. If so, they would profit by $140 to $240 million annually from a one billion gallon larger subsidized ethanol market.

port subsidy and promotion programs and would help forestall wasteful regulation aimed at wildlife protection and other environmental objectives. But one cannot be sure without much more thorough benefit-cost analysis than has been carried out to date.

Market Stabilization. A traditional purpose of governmental intervention in commodity markets is price stabilization. A policy option for focusing commodity programs on stabilization would be to increase the market orientation of the farmer-owned-reserve program by giving farmers complete freedom to decide when to store or to withdraw commodities and to widen the program beyond grains but keep strict upper limits on quantities permitted to receive storage or interest-rate subsidies. The main element of such an option would be to convert the deficiency payment, dairy, and other programs to strictly stabilization purposes. Senator J. Robert Kerrey has proposed, to this end, reducing deficiency payments for grains by fifty to sixty cents a bushel and increasing loan rates by the same amount (*Omaha World Herald*, September 21, 1994). I shall consider that proposal and then a more general stabilization option.

The Kerrey plan for grain market stabilization. Reducing deficiency payments fifty cents a bushel is taken to mean reducing target prices by that amount. For corn that would imply a target price of $2.25; and raising the loan rate by fifty cents gives a level of $2.39. For wheat the target price would be $3.50 and the loan rate $3.08. I assume that when tuned more precisely, Kerrey's idea is to set the target price essentially equal to the loan rate, at a level equal to the expected market price, and to have acreage reduction programs be triggered by stock-use ratios as in current law.

One advantage of Kerrey's plan is that grain deficiency payments would end, so that we would realize budget savings of about $5 billion annually. Another advantage is that the Commodity Credit Corporation stocks acquired in large-crop years would stabilize prices.

A disadvantage of Kerrey's plan is that farm income would fall. In addition, consumer prices of grain-containing products, notably meat, would rise. Finally, Commodity Credit Corporation stocks would likely become wastefully large and would trigger larger acreage reduction programs than under current policy; but participation might be too low for acreage reduction programs to be effective.

Analysis. Kerrey's proposal essentially replaces a complex program transferring several billion dollars annually to owners of grain payment bases (but without large distortion of land or other input use) by a program that provides half or less the income support to producers but encourages larger acreage and other input use in response to the support price (because the program supports the market price).

The market effects would depend on how acreage reduction programs are handled. Assume first that acreage reduction programs would remain at the 5.0 to 7.5 percent levels of the USDA Economic Research Service and Food and Agricultural Policy Research Institute baselines. That would imply expected market-clearing corn prices from 1996 through 1998 of about $2.25 for the year-average price received by farmers and a $3.20 price of wheat. Commodity Credit Corporation loan rates of $2.39 and $3.21 for corn and wheat, respectively, would raise the expected market return by roughly the value of an at-the-money put option for wheat and the price of corn by the value of a put in the money by fourteen cents per bushel. On the basis of the volatility of annual-average prices in recent years, we should expect farmers to produce corn and wheat in quantities called forth by prices about 10 percent above baseline prices for corn and 5 percent for wheat. With absolute-value elasticities of supply and demand that sum to about .8 for corn and 1.2 for wheat, we would expect to see Commodity Credit Corporation stock accumulation, on average from 1996 through 1998, of about 6 percent of wheat production (150 million bushels) and of about 8 percent of corn production (600 million bushels) each year. Thus, the expected level of Commodity Credit Corporation stocks would soon become burdensome.

With stock-based acreage reduction program triggers, excess supplies could be tempered. With deficiency payments gone, however, the only reason for program participation is eligibility for Commodity Credit Corporation loans—a benefit farmers are unlikely to view as worth even a 5 percent acreage reduction program, much less 7.5 percent. So unless new participation incentives such as "green" payments are added, the Kerrey plan is very likely to require a paid acreage diversion program to avoid large government-held stockholdings. Such a program might indeed be an attractive substitute for deficiency payments. For example, paying $100 per acre rent on 10 percent of the roughly seventy-five million corn acres would cost the Treasury $750 million annually—less than half of baseline deficiency payments for corn.

Assuming effective acreage controls that permit the market price to be higher than the baseline price, consumers will lose from the Kerrey plan. And, unless diversion payments are large enough, farmers will be worse off also.

For a U.S. aggregate accounting, the issue is whether government budget savings are greater than the consumer and producer losses, and that turns on which approach has greater dead-weight losses. Neither case affords a simple measure of that loss. The main component is the opportunity cost of idled acreage. We expect that to be higher under the Kerrey plan because the expected market price is higher, and current deficiency payments are largely decoupled from farms' acreage and other input decisions.

The further issue is what net stabilization benefits we can expect from the government's management of stocks under the Kerrey plan. I would place the net benefits at about zero. That is optimistic, given past Commodity Credit Corporation performance. But I assume that the new, higher loan rates will be established by a farmer-owned-reserve mechanism closer to a simple storage subsidy to private inventory holders, with no specified "release" prices, than to past government stockholding policies.

Therefore, I expect that the Kerrey plan would be only marginally worse than current policies.

The farm income stabilization option. This option would have several features. Target prices for grain and cotton would be set for three-year periods, at the baseline market price for that period, with payment bases updated to 85 percent of 1992 through 1994 average output. In addition, loan rates would remain at current levels. The milk support price and Commodity Credit Corporation purchases would be replaced by a deficiency payment scheme with the target price initially at $10.10 and after three years adopting the grains procedure; the payment quantity would be frozen at 85 percent of actual 1993 through 1994 average sales. The oilseed, sugar, peanut, and tobacco programs would be converted to a similar approach. Finally, all acreage reduction programs, marketing loans, advance deficiency payments, and payment limits would end.

The baseline prices used would be the same as those now used in budget scoring. But because agreement on baseline prices would become even more important, an institutional arrangement would be established in which

139

the CBO and the General Accounting Office would col-
laborate with the OMB and the USDA in developing the
baseline.

To see how the program would work, consider corn
for the period 1996 through 1998. Suppose that the baseline corn price arrived at was $2.05 for that period.[12] Then
the target price would be $2.05. Suppose that the season-
average price of corn turned out to be $2.00. The U.S.
payment base would be about 7.5 billion bushels (85 percent of 1992 through 1994 U.S. production). Deficiency
payments would be $375 million.

If the season-average price were above $2.05, there
would be no payments. By construction, payments at
baseline prices would be zero. With budget scoring that
uses baseline prices, that program would be scored to
have zero outlays.

The spirit of that program is similar to the 1994 crop
disaster insurance program, which automatically pays
indemnities to program-crop producers whose yields fall
below 50 percent of average and are in a county where
the yield is below 65 percent of its average.[13] But the
"price insurance" has no individual-farm trigger, has no
deductible (payments accrue for any shortfall below the
baseline price), and involves no fee from producers.[14]

---

12. That is ten cents lower than current USDA or Food and Agricultural Policy Research Institute baselines, because for purposes of
this program, which has no acreage reduction programs, we need a
zero acreage reduction program baseline, while current-policy baselines have 5 to 10 percent acreage reduction programs.

13. See the monograph by Barry K. Goodwin and Vincent H.
Smith, *The Economics of Crop Insurance and Disaster Aid*, in the AEI
Studies in Agricultural Policy.

14. A more drastic version of that reform would have a deductible and would charge a fee. For example, payments might be made
only if the market price falls below 90 percent of the baseline price,
and a fee, say $5 per acre, might be charged. That version of the pro-
gram would be equivalent to the government's selling put options
with a strike price at 90 percent of the baseline price. That highlights
a parallel to the options pilot programs that have been carried out

While such a stabilization option, in any of the versions mentioned, would be scored at zero budget outlays, expected outlays would, of course, not be zero. Prices are sure to be below the baseline in many years for many commodities and thus would trigger payments, while prices above the baseline would not trigger savings. Scoring conventions have been modified to give budget costs to disaster programs, and it would make sense to undertake probabilistic or statistical scoring for the stabilization option also. The CBO is said to be considering such an approach even for existing price support programs. Implementation would be a formidable task, but probably easier than the environmental benefit-cost scoring that will have to be undertaken at some stage. The costs of ignoring the issue are too large to do nothing.

The advantages of the stabilization option are that it eliminates the dead-weight losses from acreage idling and the distortions of farmers' production choices and that it affords budget savings of about $9 billion annually. In addition, that option stabilizes markets more predictably and uniformly across producers.

One disadvantage of the stabilization option is that farmers give up about $9 billion annually in payments, and farm income declines (but by much less than $9 billion). In addition, payment-base asset values decline—a loss to landowners. Finally, such sweeping changes raise major implementation issues.

Analysis. This option is a more substantial revision of programs than any of the others considered earlier. The details require a lot of working out, especially for

---

under the 1985 and 1990 farm acts. The pilot programs involved highly subsidized puts that are far in the money, for example, guaranteeing a sale of corn at $2.75 when the expected market price is $2.20. The new "put options" considered here would have a smaller subsidy of the premium on an out-of-the-money put.

the nondeficiency payment commodities. The option could be implemented for deficiency payment commodities only, but there is an important equity issue in leaving untouched the commodities—sugar, peanuts, and tobacco—that get their support directly from the pockets of consumers rather than through government payments.

The basic idea of such an option is that it could accomplish more for taxpayers and consumers than the earlier across-the-board target price cuts, while at the same time costing farmers less. The reason is that target price cuts would still leave the structure of current programs intact and would retain the distortions and inefficiencies that are especially burdensome for those commodities without a deficiency-payment program. The stabilization option, which removes existing constraints, would fit well with shifting the federal government's efforts toward industrial policies that meet a benefit-cost test for investment in environmental improvement, research and information, technological developments in new uses of farm products, and market stabilization. The international economic environment that will emerge under the new GATT agreement, the NAFTA, and free trade negotiations yet to come is better suited to a prosperous agriculture under the industrial policy option than under current farm programs.

12
Recommendations

Recommendations on policy options require overarching criteria by which they may be judged. That is to say, what do we want farm programs for anyway? What is their purpose? Even with agreement on basic purposes, many of the most contentious issues involve trade-offs among economic interests—program participants versus taxpayers who pay for the programs, equity in program benefits among producers of different commodities. Those trade-offs are ultimately a political matter to which economists have little to contribute beyond pointing out that dead-weight losses of economic distortions make it inevitable that the gainers will gain less than the losers will lose from government intervention. But unless one is willing to make judgments about the value of transferring a dollar from, say, an average taxpayer to an average wheat grower, one cannot make the call on how the pros and cons of wheat policy alternatives add up.

A key overarching economic issue for farm policy choice in 1995 is whether we (as a society represented by Congress) want our farm policy to be welfare policy or industrial policy. Farm policy as welfare policy involves redistributing income from one group of people to another. Farm policy as industrial policy involves efforts to make the farm economy, and hence the U.S. economy, work better, through investment in public goods, improvement of the environment, or correction of other market failures.

I believe that experience with farm programs indi-

143

cates that we ought to move away from farm policy as welfare policy. The reason is that majority support for welfare policy requires that the beneficiaries be needy and deserving—having suffered harm not their fault. But while rural areas have needy people, they are not the beneficiaries of farm commodity programs. They do not produce enough that even high prices would solve their problems. On the other hand, commercial-scale farmers on average have income and wealth well above the U.S. average; and the minority of farms at risk of business failure through large debts and low returns are not plausibly assisted through price supports that provide windfalls to the majority of farmers, bid up land values, and engender commodity surpluses. Those farms need individual financial attention, after which they should be reinvigorated or placed under new management.

The rejection of farm policy as welfare leaves us with the industrial policy issues. Impartial observers indeed have found social goods for agricultural legislation to address: market stabilization, research, food safety, and environmental improvement. Again, however, experience shows us that the sixty-year vigorous pursuit of interest-group agendas has largely coopted the social goods hoped for. By now most of us know that farm policy, whatever its public-interest wrappings, generates market-distorting intervention that predictably yields results counterproductive to the well-being of the nation as a whole.

That has led me to consider successively less marginal and more radical options for the 1995 farm bill and finally to endorse the relatively modest intervention of the pure stabilization option, supplemented with limited public investment in environmental, food safety, informational, and research activities and continuing government efforts to open markets for U.S. farm products abroad. Each of those areas, however, requires careful assessment on its own terms. That is what the legislative hearing process for the 1995 farm bill should be all about.

References

Alston, Julian M., and Brian H. Hurd. "Some Neglected Social Costs of Government Spending in Farm Programs." *American Journal of Agricultural Economics* 72 (February 1990): 149–56.

Alston, Julian M., and Philip G. Pardey. *Making Science Pay: The Economics of Agricultural R&D Policy.* Washington, D.C.: AEI Press, 1995.

Barr, James C. Testimony on H.R. 2664: The Milk Producers Self-Help Program. House Committee on Agriculture, Subcommittee on Livestock, July 21, 1993.

Congressional Budget Office. "Reducing the Deficit: Spending and Revenue Option." Washington, D.C.: Government Printing Office, March 1994.

Crittenden, Ann. *Killing the Sacred Cows.* New York: Penguin, 1993.

Dairy Policy Task Force. "Federal Milk Marketing Orders." American Agricultural Economic Association Occasional Paper No. 3, June 1986.

Food and Agricultural Policy Institute. *FAPRI 1994 International Agricultural Outlook.* Staff Report #2–94. Iowa State University and University of Missouri, May 1994.

Gardner, Bruce L. "The United States." In *Agricultural Protectionism in the Industrialized World,* edited by F. H. Sanderson. Washington, D.C.: Resources for the Future, 1991.

Goodwin, Barry K., and Vincent H. Smith. *The Economics of Crop Insurance and Disaster Aid.* Washington, D.C.: AEI Press, 1995.

Halcrow, Harold G. *Food Policy for America.* New York: McGraw-Hill, 1977.

Lin, William. "Aggregate Effects of Commodity Programs." USDA-ERS mimeo. Washington, D.C.: U.S. Department of Agriculture, 1989.

Thurman, Walter N. *Assessing the Environmental Impact of Farm Policies.* Washington, D.C.: AEI Press, 1995.

U.S. Department of Agriculture. *National Financial Summary, 1991.* Economic Research Service, ECIFS-11–1, January 1993a.

U.S. Department of Agriculture. "Long-Term Agricultural Baseline Projections." World Agricultural Outlook Board, WAOB-93–1, October 1993b.

U.S. Department of Agriculture. *News.* Release No. 0149.94, February 25, 1994a.

U.S. Department of Agriculture. *Wheat: Commodity Fact Sheet.* Farm Service Agency, November 1994b.

U.S. Department of Agriculture. *Agricultural Outlook.* Economic Research Service, AO-214, December 1994c.

Westcott, Paul C. "Market-Oriented Agriculture." USDA-ERS, Agricultural Economic Report No. 671, June 1993.

Index

About the Authors

BRIAN D. WRIGHT is professor of agricultural and resource economics at the University of California at Berkeley. He has also served on the faculties of Yale University and Harvard University. Mr. Wright is coauthor of *Storage and Commodity Markets* and has published more than forty academic articles. He is a reviewer for many economics journals and the National Science Foundation and is a consultant to the World Bank and other institutions. He has served as an expert witness in legal proceedings. His professional interests include public economics, agricultural policy, trade, financial markets, research and development, market organization and behavior, antitrust theory, and commodity market stabilization.

BRUCE L. GARDNER is professor of agricultural and resource economics at the University of Maryland at College Park. He served as assistant secretary for economics in the U.S. Department of Agriculture from 1989 through 1991 and was a senior staff economist at the President's Council of Economic Advisers from 1975 through 1977. He has also been professor of agricultural economics at Texas A&M University and North Carolina State University and a visiting fellow at the Center for the Study of the Economy and the State at the University of Chicago. Mr. Gardner's professional writings and research have focused on agricultural commodity policy, food marketing, trade and environment, farm labor, population, crop insurance, and futures and commodity options in agriculture. He is the author of *The Economics of Agricultural Policies*, *The Governing of Agriculture*, and *Optimal Stockpiling of Grain*.

153

A Note on the Book

*This book was edited by Leigh Tripoli
of the publications staff
of the American Enterprise Institute.
Hördur Karlsson drew the figures.
Robert Elwood prepared the index.
The text was set in Palatino, a typeface
designed by the twentieth-century Swiss designer
Hermann Zapf. Coghill Composition of Richmond, Virginia, set the
type, and Edwards Brothers Incorporated of Lillington, North Carolina,
using permanent acid-free paper, printed and bound the book.*

The AEI Press is the publisher for the American Enterprise Institute
for Public Policy Research, 1150 Seventeenth Street, N.W., Washington, D.C. 20036; *Christopher DeMuth*, publisher; *Dana Lane*, director; *Ann Petty*, editor; *Leigh Tripoli*, editor; *Cheryl Weissman*, editor; *Lisa Roman*, editorial assistant (rights and permissions).